A PERFECT SEASON

Darryl Belfry

To Nick & Michael

Best of luck.

Trafford
PUBLISHING

Order this book online at www.trafford.com/07-0995
or email orders@trafford.com

Most Trafford titles are also available at major online book retailers.

Edited by David & Liz Thomson
Photography by Lisa Ip-Eizenga

Note for Librarians: A cataloguing record for this book is available from Library
and Archives Canada at www.collectionscanada.ca/amicus/index-e.html

Printed in Victoria, BC, Canada.

ISBN: 978-1-4251-2849-4

*We at Trafford believe that it is the responsibility of us all, as both individuals
and corporations, to make choices that are environmentally and socially sound.
You, in turn, are supporting this responsible conduct each time you purchase a
Trafford book, or make use of our publishing services. To find out how you are
helping, please visit www.trafford.com/responsiblepublishing.html*

*Our mission is to efficiently provide the world's finest, most comprehensive
book publishing service, enabling every author to experience success.
To find out how to publish your book, your way, and have it available
worldwide, visit us online at www.trafford.com/10510*

 www.trafford.com

North America & international
toll-free: 1 888 232 4444 (USA & Canada)
phone: 250 383 6864 ♦ fax: 250 383 6804 ♦ email: info@trafford.com

The United Kingdom & Europe
phone: +44 (0)1865 722 113 ♦ local rate: 0845 230 9601
facsimile: +44 (0)1865 722 868 ♦ email: info.uk@trafford.com

10 9 8 7 6 5 4 3 2

DEDICATION

I dedicate this book to Albert "Bud" Chenard,

Thank you for being my mentor and believing in me. Your magical approach to teaching gave me the voice to deliver my message. In writing this book, I hope to ignite the passion of teaching to every coach who aspires to make a difference.

Your friend,
Darryl

TABLE OF CONTENTS

FOREWORD

"A PERFECT SEASON" is an instructional book intended to convey over 30 individual and team development strategies for minor hockey coaches, parents and players.

At the heart of the book is the "Triangle Approach." The Triangle Approach to coaching is to personalize the experience for each player and to UPLIFT, ENABLE and INSPIRE, which serves the coach as a compass guiding his every decision.

"A Perfect Season" provides a season plan reference for coaches, a development template for Minor Hockey Associations, a resource for parents and inspiration for young hockey players.

I wish all the best to those of you who strive for *the Perfect Season.*

Darryl Belfry

Acknowledgements

I HAVE BEEN blessed over the course of my life and career by the support, encouragement and faith from my family, friends, mentors, students and colleagues.

First I thank my beautiful wife, Ruth, whose love and support has inspired me to strive every day to realize my potential and to take time to enjoy the "little things".

I thank my daughter, Ella, who is the light in my life.

A very special thanks to Albert "Bud" Chenard, who was the first one to show faith in an inexperienced twenty-one year old who had to first teach himself to skate. Then stand by me when he didn't have the time, the health, or the energy to.

My dad, Roger, who told me when I first started, "Just because that's the way they have always done it, doesn't mean you can't change it." His words of support gave me the courage to be different.

I thank my wonderful editors, David and Liz Thomson, who without their guidance, patience and expertise this book would not have been possible. Lisa Ip-Eizenga, my photographer, who took my exact vision for the cover and brought it to life.

This page is not big enough for me to properly thank all of my students, past and present, each of you continue to challenge me in ways I never thought possible. Your honest work ethic gives me the daily pleasure of one of life's greatest gifts...the privilege to teach motivated young people.

To all of you, I give my thanks.

INTRODUCTION

EVERY COACH HAS the choice to be remembered fondly, or to be quickly forgotten; the difference lies in the quality of the relationship built with the student.

Minor Hockey – there may not be a more misleading term in all of sports. Anyone who has spent any time around our game knows there is nothing "minor" in Minor hockey, especially when you are a coach. Every game is very serious business.

I am amazed when I think about my early days as a minor hockey coach and think how my priorities, my attitudes and my thoughts about development evolved ... especially that first year. I was fortunate to have the opportunity to coach many great players, and have several great teachers whose teachings left an indelible impression. I wasn't very different from most adults who coach young people in that I really wanted to make a difference and to impart some 'special knowledge' that would serve the player for years to come. I learned that the art of coaching is about personalizing the experience.

Coaching hockey is a wonderful opportunity to make a positive impact in the lives of young people and I hope this story will inspire you to rise to the challenge!

Apart from the introduction, the book is a fictional novel, told from the perspective of an average, everyday minor hockey coach, as he relives the lessons and specific strategies that helped him fulfill his coaching purpose.

Every season the success or failure of the coach comes down to a series of interactions with his players. Coaches who aspire to create new levels of performance, commitment and understanding must focus on outcomes that uplift, enable and inspire their individual players and the team collectively. The way coaches manage these teaching moments will either build the bridge to development—or burn it.

UPLIFT, ENABLE and INSPIRE is what I refer to as 'The Triangle Approach' which is the guiding principle of this book and the coaching compass that will lead you to A PERFECT SEASON.

Your role as a coach is to create successful situations for your players in an effort to develop inner confidence (Uplift); to provide a progressive and challenging skill and tactical development program that highlights strengths and provides opportunity to improve areas of opportunity (Enable); to personalize the experience in a way that each of your players feels accepted, believes his or her role on the team is valued, and senses a genuine concern for him or her as an individual (Inspire). When you perform your role according to the Triangle Approach, your team is poised for a Perfect Season.

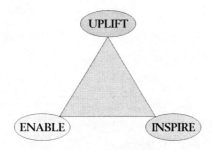

COACHING CHALLENGES:
Throughout the novel, I illustrate various challenges that the coach and his team must overcome. At the end of each chapter I include a 'Coaching Challenge' as a chance for you to relate the story to your own experiences and apply the strategies to your own team situation. I would encourage you to take a few minute to complete the 'Coaching Challenges' as they come up during the book.

I dedicate this book to all coaches who are motivated to turn every year into the "Perfect Season".

1

THE END...FIRST

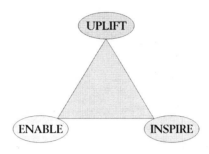

STRATEGY #1: COACH TO MAKE A DIFFERENCE

Discover as much reward in the development process of each player as you do in the competitive results of your team.

WHEN MY WIFE and I married, and planned for a family of our own, I had to make several changes in my life. The decision to give up coaching was not easy because I had learned to appreciate the many valuable lessons of the experience.

During my absence from hockey, I remember wondering what coaching impact I had made. Early on I was more of a student than a teacher. I learned just as much, if not more, from the players as they did from me.

When I first started coaching, I focused on building a winning program. I thought creating "championship" experiences was the best way to be remembered. I wanted a trophy to remind the players of our success. As my coaching evolved, the number of ways I measured success evolved as well, and I began to find great enjoyment in the process of coaching. I started to take more pride in building relationships with my players, creating team unity, and overcoming obstacles – and to place less emphasis on the competitive result.

I thought about my own life. I thought about how my trophies have spent more time in a box in the attic, than reminding me of the great teams and coaches for whom I had played. The memories I have of my coaches resonate in my coaching attitude, style and practices. The aspects of their coaching that I liked, respected and responded to, I have adopted or adapted into my own coaching style.

However, for all coaches, the purest measure of coaching success comes from the reaction of a former player who recognizes you in a chance meeting, in a most unlikely time and place.

For me, my moment came when I was walking through the mall with my wife during the holidays, and I heard someone yell through the crowd.

"Hey Coach!"

My wife and I turned towards the sound to see a young man pushing his way through the crowd and coming in our direction.

"Hey Coach!"

When he finally got to us, he asked with a smile, "Remember me?"

I will not forget that team or any of those players as long as I live. I coached them for three years and made a point to follow each of them as they left town to pursue all levels of hockey from Junior B to Pro.

"It's me coach! Sammy", he said.

"Hey Sammy, how are you doing?" I asked excitedly.

"Great coach, how are you?" He said, nearly shouting.

Before I had a chance to respond, he continued proudly ... "I'm in school Coach. I got a scholarship to play hockey down in the States and I'm home for Christmas."

"That's awesome! We knew you could do it." I said, as I extended my hand in congratulations.

"I can save a couple complimentary tickets for you at the will call, anytime you want to come to a game," he offered eagerly. "Hey coach, what's Bud up to?" He asked.

Bud had been my beloved assistant coach. We are great friends. Over the years he has been my greatest teacher and every player that played for us absolutely adored him.

"Yeah, I see him all the time. He's doing well. I will mention the game to him. I am sure he would love to come," I said reassuringly.

He made a point to thank me for encouraging him to be a student-athlete the first year we had the team.

"I would never have pursued the scholarship without you," Sammy added.

We talked about "The SEASON" and caught up on where teammates are now playing. We reminisced fondly about that wonderful season that changed so many of us. In closing, Sammy promised he would email me so we could keep in touch.

As he shook my hand again, he thanked me for the hundredth time, then apologized to my wife for interrupting our shopping day, and then sincerely invited her to come to a game as well. She smiled and thanked him politely.

When he walked in the opposite direction, I still felt the adrenaline from the chance meeting. I was on cloud nine. You could not have wiped the smile off my face. I felt an overwhelming sense of pride when this former player had recognized me, and had taken the time to come over and thank me. It was amazing. I hope I never take those moments for granted. It was special to cross paths with a player years after I had coached him. For him to both take the time and make the effort to come and see me meant he remembered me, and the impression I made must have been positive and long lasting. The rush was as high as winning the games. Moments like these are what coaching is all about and I consider them the final measure of success.

My wife was watching me, and a couple minutes later asked, "Who was that?"

Who was that? I thought. Where do I start?

Sammy was a player on a team that left a lasting imprint on all those who had the privilege to be a part of it.

I think I always hoped that I had made a positive impression on my players, but how could I really know?

Before that season, I thought coaching hockey was actually about hockey. However, my perspective changed that year and I learned that skills and strategy are not the most important focus. Coaching is about building relationships. Without the relationship with the student, the teacher has no medium to drive home his message.

I no longer view myself as just a hockey coach, I am more like a teacher by trade and interest; I teach life skills through a common interest in the game of hockey.

More importantly, I have learned that coaching can make a difference.

COACHING CHALLENGE #1: LEGACY

1. What do you hold as your greatest coaching achievement?
2. Why is that achievement so special to you?
3. What do you want your players to remember from their experience with you as their coach?

2

THE BEGINNING

STRATEGY #2: LEAD FROM BEHIND

Control for a coach comes from accountability. You will find no greater accountability measure for your team than the one those you are leading prescribe for themselves.

I KNEW MY last year of university marked the end of my playing career. I loved hockey at every level and I had considered myself lucky to have played for excellent coaches along the way. I felt strongly that it was time to give something back to a game that had been so good to me.

I decided I wanted to coach in Minor Hockey. I had no previous coaching experience other than helping at a couple hockey schools. The hockey school experience was great but brief. Unlike developing a team from start to finish over the course of nine months the hockey school format was designed to teach or instruct only for a couple weeks. I wanted to get more involved with hockey development.

I had met John, the association's Director of Coach and Player Development, or "coach for the coaches" as he was referred to. During my coach selection interview I learned that John was in his mid-thirties and had acquired an impressive coaching background from youth to Junior.

My first impression of John was that he was very passionate about the process of coaching. What I found most interesting was how much time we spent discussing things like team building, teaching style, learning environment and preparation. By the end of the interview, I came away feeling like we were two old friends meeting for a cup of coffee and talking hockey. I really liked his approach. John turned a typically dry and uninspiring question and answer format into a passionate hockey discussion where I felt completely at ease.

I was feeling a little nervous heading into my first year of coaching and was excited when John called to invite me to attend a pre-season coaches' meeting.

The meeting intrigued me. I found it odd that we were meeting in the spring when the season was so far away. The approach seemed unconventional, yet I was happy to go, even if it was just to meet the other coaches.

The Association Plan

John opened the meeting with an interesting statement that changed my perspective or philosophy of a minor hockey coach.

"Congratulations, you have all made the team, the most important team in the Association. The coaches in this association work together. We share ideas, we share drills, we lend our time, and we mentor and support one another. I am the Head Coach of this team of coaches and I want to welcome you to our team."

I don't know what the other coaches expected coming into the meeting, but I don't think any of us expected a statement quite like that. We all came from an era of 'Island Coaches,' where the coach went into seclusion for the season and no one heard from him unless he was defending himself and his coaching practices in a discipline meeting. If the coach wanted new ideas, they took it upon themselves to go to coaching clinics and seminars, to talk to other coaches and steal from other coaches. However, I had never heard of a structured learning and support program put forth by the association to educate and align its coaches to a progressive teaching system.

John proceeded to explain that 'our team' would be designing an association development plan. Essentially, we were going to identify the core skills, tactics, and strategies for the association. If implemented in proper sequence, our core curriculum would provide players with the opportunity to choose the level of competition they wished to pursue.

With each passing year, the demand for skill increases at the elite level of the sport. Unfortunately too many good athletes never get the chance to develop at an elite level. Blame it on poor skill development planning during the formative years or just blame it on poor coaching. Many athletes never have the choice to train at the elite level. Essentially the choice is made for them.

John stated the mission of the association was to ensure that no player would graduate from our program without having had the opportunity to acquire the skills to compete at the next level. If the player chose not to work hard, not to commit to excellence and simply chose to play recreationally, there was nothing wrong with that; at least they had that choice to make.

Our first challenge as a team of coaches would be to work together to create the development plan. It became clear to each coach that John wanted us to buy into having a plan. He knew that if he created it on his own and handed us a manual at the start of the season he would have an uphill battle. However, if he included us in the process, we would naturally buy in because we would want to see our ideas come to fruition.

The more we engaged in the tasks and the conversations the more I found John's leadership style coming to the forefront. It was interesting to watch his approach and participate in the exercises. We had some wonderful discussions and debates about development principles, which I found educational. I felt we were starting to come together as a team.

John was leading from behind. He was working to let the ideas flow from the group and then he would take the ideas and help us arrange them into patterns and progressions. He would challenge us on critical points of interest, play "devil's advocate", and allow for positive debate. In the end, when we viewed the final product, it was a collective philosophy rather than a dictated policy. John masterfully put his stamp on our association that day, and his approach earned the respect of the entire group as he invited us all to become part of the process.

He said something interesting at the beginning of the meeting that day that I think captures the essence of what he was trying to achieve and what role he was trying to have as the coach of our team.

He told a story about a great sculptor, who was creating his artwork from stone with a chisel. The townspeople marveled at the quality of the work, the artistry was beyond words and the attention to detail was nothing like anyone had ever seen before. When one of the townspeople asked him how he could create such a magnificent masterpiece, the sculptor replied that the masterpiece was always inside the rock. All he did was 'chip' away the pieces that covered it up.

This parable perfectly described John's leadership style and illustrated the importance for all coaches to look for the potential in their players and guide them to find their own way. He repeatedly said, "The role of the coach is to UPLIFT, ENABLE and INSPIRE their athletes."

That day, he was able to UPLIFT, ENABLE and INSPIRE all of us, by guiding us to map the blueprint for our success. At the end of the meeting when we viewed our work, we were so proud of what we had created. It truly was always there; John just created the environment and guided us in a way that pulled it out. That is leading from behind.

COACHING CHALLENGE #2: LEADING FROM BEHIND

1. Can you remember a time when someone led you from behind and took the role of guiding you to find your own way?
2. List three ways you can apply this strategy to your team.
3. List three benefits that could come from this approach.

3

SEASON PLANNING

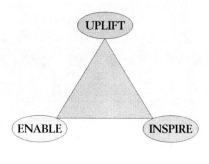

STRATEGY #3: PLAN TO TEACH

Lasting and impacting development is progressive. Identify the elements that must be taught and teach them in order.

THEY SAY A team takes on the personality of its coach. I believe that day our coaches unknowingly adopted John's style of leadership. I know many of us used that style in our own teams, and found the players respond brilliantly as they took responsibility for their development and became accountable to themselves and each other. Authentic responsibility and accountability is born from participation in the process.

Many coaches take the dictator approach, "I am the boss and you are going to do what I say."

When accountability and responsibility is forced it results in low levels of motivation and creativity, which jeopardizes the growth and development of the player.

Have you ever asked a team to create a set of rules and consequences for those rules? I am always astonished when I do that now. The kids always create many more rules and much more severe consequences for themselves than coaches would ever dream. When players share in the process, things like commitment and accountability shift from being elusive to becoming cornerstones of the identity of the team.

"I am trying to create a development program for the entire association that links one level to the next, much the same as the school system. I am tired of hearing coaches walk into the locker room to start the season and say. Forget what you learned and how you played last year. This year you are going to learn to play my way. I believe every year should build on the development of the one before," John said, stating his position.

"What we want to do is create a core curriculum to form the foundation of development in the association. Development will be a set of measurable objectives that you as the coach must achieve throughout the season. The remainder of the development time is free for you, the coach, to put your personal stamp on the hockey team. This way, we know that whatever else we teach we will all achieve our core objectives each year. That assures me of achieving my personal mandate for the association," John concluded.

By the end of the process, I understood my mandate and had a plan to implement development into my season.

My Peewee team represents the first years of the Performance Stream on our Association Development Plan. These are critical years for the players to learn a few core skills and tactics in preparation for competition with the best of their age group.

SKILLS:

1. Each player's season ending test results must rank in the top half of the Minor Bantam's preseason test results, indicating a clear core skill graduation to the next level.
2. Each player is introduced to a personalized strength and conditioning program with a structure to record improvement in core strength and recovery conditioning.
3. All players must have a complete understanding of their Player Profile (strengths and weaknesses) as well as a firm grasp of how they can consistently apply their strengths in game situations.

TACTICS:

1. Each player will have the ability to rotate, adjust and interchange positions without hesitation.
2. Each player will have the ability to create offensive opportunities off the rush and in down low situations.

3. Each player will have the ability to make in-game strategic adjustments and specific opponent adjustments.

TEAM BUILDING
1. The team will have clear team identity.
2. The team will have consistent team rituals.
3. The team will have a scheduled team building exercise each month of the season.

These requirements represent my minimum standard of achievement as a coach; anything I can teach beyond these objectives is at my personal discretion. My team must be prepared to play at the next level before they get there.

It was interesting to see how each team fit into a development stream and each level presented its own challenges that influenced its development mandate. The Atom AAA team, for example, is part of the Teaching Stream and their mandate included time and space, space and area passes, recognize and skate the puck into open ice, pin and contain, develop a quick release shot and create triangles.

"Your success lies in your ability to prepare your team to compete the following year," John said.

"We're trying to build something here and each season represents a critical building block that creates a foundation for us to grow closer to our goal," John said passionately.

"When you look at it from that perspective, you can see how important it is that specific goals are achieved each season."

It was a great process. John had a wealth of information and I was continually impressed by how detailed his vision for the association was. It was inspiring to know that I was part of a master development plan that encompassed the entire association. With tryouts just around the corner, I could hardly contain my enthusiasm.

COACHING CHALLENGE #3: A PLAN FOR DEVELOPMENT

Please consider the following questions:

1. What is your development mandate? If you don't have one from your association, what points of development are necessary for your team this year?
2. Have you seen the next level for your team? (The team one year older)

What are the characteristics that will be important for them to be successful?

3. How can you integrate the 'next level' skills and tactics into your program to prepare your team for the demands of the next level?

Support Staff:

The last topic of discussion for this part of the process was support staff.

John opened the discussion by stating the obvious.

"The approach to communicating with kids as a minor hockey coach has changed from when most of us played. Coaching in today's era is different and your willingness to adjust will largely determine whether you will be successful."

What came next was not as obvious.

"I have identified a player's perspective that I hope will be helpful to understand how to communicate with today's young people with the hope that you keep this in mind when you are recruiting your staff."

John then distributed the following article he had written.

COACHING APPROACH FROM THE PLAYER'S PERSPECTIVE

1. I respond to people I like.

   Your resume might be impressive to my parents and the people who selected you for this position, but I don't care where you played or what you did in the past. My reaction to you is based on personal experience. If you want me to respond to you, I need to believe that you genuinely care about me. If I do not think you care about me, I will not care about what you have to say.

2. If it is not fun, I will not try my best, and when I get the chance to choose to do something else, I will.

   Coach, hockey is one of a thousand things I could be doing with my time. If it is not fun and rewarding for me, the first chance I have the option of doing something else, I will. I need to know that you want me on this team. I need an environment that makes me feel comfortable to be myself, and I need to know I am getting better.

3. I need to know why or I probably will not put much effort into it.

> If you are not forthcoming with the reason why it is important for us to do what you want us to do, I will ask you. I need to know why because I do not like to waste my time. If you do not have a good reason, you will not get a good effort. If it is that important to you, you will have a reason why. By the way coach, don't try to fluff me off with a casual answer because I will see right through it.

After reviewing the "Coaching Approach" passage, the group engaged in discussion. There are a few points that struck a chord with me that I want to point out to you.

1. Your goal in recruiting your staff is to surround yourself with people with whom you can work and people who can communicate and identify well with the kids on your team. Remember your responsibility as the leader of the team is to look for ways to UPLIFT, ENABLE and INSPIRE your athletes.
2. If most kids learn best through imitation and no one on your coaching staff can offer a quality physical example of what you are trying to teach, have you surrounded yourself with the best possible staff? The staff with the most hockey coaching experience may not be as effective in teaching skills as the one who has included someone who can provide quality physical examples of the skills you are trying to teach.

John left us with one final thought, "The point I want each of you to remember when recruiting your staff is that the message you are trying to convey to your players means little if the messenger cannot communicate effectively with the student."

The message 'rang loud and clear' through the room; it is important that we take some time to think about how and who is going to convey our message. Kids identify with different people and the more diverse a staff we can put together, the better chance we have of reaching all the players on our team.

4

UNEXPECTED TEACHABLE MOMENT

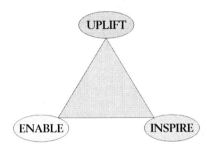

STRATEGY #4: THE BEST TEACHING MOMENTS COME AT UNEXPECTED TIMES

Create a habit of engaging in conversation with your players, many times simply asking a question to a young player will lead you into a perfect teaching moment.

AFTER THE MEETING, I left not knowing exactly who to pick for my assistants. The truth was I had no idea where to look for the staff or the support with which John wanted us to surround ourselves.

I was planning to wait until after I had selected the team to seek help within the parent group. If I approached any parents prior to this stage, I would be selecting nearly a third of my team before tryouts. I would lose credibility before the season even started. I was dumbfounded; I mean where were we going to find these people? Moreover, how was I supposed to get them to volunteer their time?

I did not know where to look, so I was idle for the first month. I talked to a few people that I knew around the usual hockey circles to get a feel for who might be out there that I should talk to, but that didn't get me too far.

I was running out of ideas, so I decided to call Coach Stone to get his thoughts. Coach Stone was my former University coach, a man for whom I had great respect, as he was a players' coach. In all of my time playing for him, I felt like he valued me on the team even though I was not one of his top performers.

He used to say, "Your job is to pay attention to the details of the game and give an effort your mom would be proud of every time you step on the ice. My job is to make sure that your attention and effort translates into improvement."

Coach Stone was a philosophical person; he always had quotations in the dressing room to make you think. I knew he was a coach that studied the game. I was certain he would have suggestions about finding good people to help me.

When I asked him his ideas for finding an assistant coach, in typical Coach Stone style, he left me with this gem:

"Look for an assistant coach much the same as you would look for a book in a bookstore. Don't go into the bookstore to choose a book. Float through the aisles with an open mind and let the book choose you. In the end the right person will emerge."

Following his advice, I put myself in the hockey environment to see if anyone would catch my attention. What better place to look than spring leagues and hockey schools, an oasis of hockey junkies? I decided to start by volunteering at one of the local hockey schools.

The second day of the hockey camp, my twelve year old "Squad" was having lunch and I noticed one of my players sitting on his own, so I joined him.

"Your name is Sean, right?" I asked striking up a conversation.

"Yes coach," he responded quietly.

"Hey Sean, are you having fun at the camp so far?" I asked hoping to get more than a one-word answer.

"Yeah, I am having fun, thanks," he said politely.

"How was your season last year Sean?" I asked curiously.

"Not too good," he answered honestly.

"Really, what happened?" I asked with concern.

"It was not as good as the year before," he said.

"Why was that?" I wondered.

"All my coach did last year was yell and scream at us. He had played pro hockey but he was not a good coach. I really didn't like him at all!" Sean elaborated.

"Wow! So it wasn't very much fun then?" I acknowledged.

"No." Sean said finally lifting his head.

As we both began to eat, there was silence between us. I was thinking hard about what to do next. I could not leave the conversation the way it was. All I could think about was John's theory on the role of the coach, to UPLIFT, ENABLE AND INSPIRE. Sean had presented me with my first opportunity to UPLIFT and INSPIRE.

I was thinking that Sean's coach probably had the best of intentions. The truth was he yelled at his players because he had run out of ideas to communicate. He masked it under the guise of "motivation," but really, he found himself caught in the emotion of the games, and allowed his frustration to become fits of temper. Sean was not inspired and certainly was not motivated.

"Hey Sean," I asked grabbing his attention.

He lifted his eyes from his plate and made eye contact before nodding.

"I had a coach like that when I played. You know the type. The one who appeared to be angry all the time," I started.

"Really?" Sean asked inquisitively.

"Yeah, I remember a couple times during the season I wanted to quit. The coach centered me out during the game for one of the mistakes that I had made and I was embarrassed," I said.

"What did you do?" Sean asked.

"Well, I talked to my Dad about it, and he told me something that I will always remember," I said leading him to the punch.

"What was that?" Sean asked with interest.

"He told me that my coach yelled at me because he didn't know what else to do. He told me he thought my coach was frustrated, and he didn't know any other way to express himself other than to yell at me. You see, Sean, when my coach yelled at me I took it personally, and I started to think the coach hated me."

"Yeah, me too," Sean said jumping in.

"Well usually, when coaches do things like that, it is not personal, even though it feels that way when it happens to you. My Dad told me when the coach yells constantly, many times he is angry with himself. He is frustrated that he doesn't have the words, or the teaching ability to help you and your teammates; maybe that's what happened to your coach last year," I said. "Let me give you an example -- imagine you want to buy a strawberry ice cream cone and when you get to the counter to buy it, the person at the counter does not speak English. You keep asking repeatedly for a strawberry ice cream cone, but the person at the counter doesn't understand, they keep pointing to every other flavor but strawberry. How frustrating would that be?" I asked.

Sean laughed, "That would be frustrating."

"So let me tell you the best part," I said trying to regain his attention.

"What's the best part?" Sean asked.

"The best part is, the very next year, a new coach took over our team, and he was one of my favorite coaches. He was completely different than the coach of the previous year."

"How?" Sean asked.

"Well, what I really liked about him was when any of us made a mistake he would never center us out in front of the team. He would pull us aside and talk to us one-on-one at the rink about things we did really well and things he'd like to see us improve on. He would also tell us how we could be better. Sometimes, when we were making the same mistake during a game, he would make up a drill about that mistake for the next practice to teach us how to do it the right way," I instructed.

"That's cool!" Sean exclaimed.

"Yeah, it was cool," I said, "I remember getting in the car after a practice that year and telling my dad how much I enjoyed playing for this coach and how much I was learning, and he turned to me with a smile and said, just think you would have missed all this if you would have quit last year."

Sean and I continued to talk about hockey and coaches until lunch was over. When we were leaving the lunch area, Sean said, "You have talked to me more today at lunch than my coach last year talked to me all season."

We shared a laugh, but Sean made a great point. Learning to communicate effectively with each of the players I am going to coach would be critical to my success. I certainly don't want any of my players to think of me, the way Sean thinks of his coach from last season.

COACHING CHALLENGE #4: UNEXPECTED TEACHING MOMENTS

1. Have you ever asked a player a simple question and you knew his or her answer presented you with an opportunity to teach?
2. There are many kids like 'Sean' in hockey, defeated by a coach who had difficulty communicating with him. When you are presented with that opportunity, what will you do to UPLIFT, ENABLE and INSPIRE?
3. Have you ever been frustrated by an inability to communicate effectively with a player? How did you overcome that obstacle?

5

STAFF RECRUITMENT

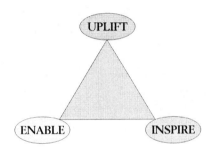

STRATEGY #5: SURROUND YOUR PLAYERS WITH THE BEST RESOURCES

Take the time to recruit complementary staff that will create value to the team, the players and be a credit to your association.

THE FIRST FEW days at the hockey school were a surprise, as I had not found the "oasis of hockey enthusiasts" that would be a great fit for my team. Discouraged and ready to give up my coaching search I started to focus on enjoying the kids for the remainder of the week. And then, I met Bud.

Bud was a man who at the time was in his mid-fifties. He had been out of hockey for a decade or more and the last thing he wanted was to get back in the game.

Thinking back on the relationship I had with Bud now I wonder how many "old hockey guys" there are in every town that have left the game for one reason or another who could serve as a mentor to young coaches. Many of these "old guys" are retired, love hockey, love kids, have a million stories to tell and are looking for a cause to champion. What could be a better cause than helping young people?

As a young coach, I needed to have the voice of experience to help me avoid making the big mistakes. I also needed someone who was going to tell me the truth when I didn't want to hear it.

Bud was standing in the corner of the rink just opposite the locker rooms. I had to walk by him to get to the instructors' locker room and when I did, I said politely, "Hi, how are you?"

"Not bad for an old guy," he quipped.

I smiled and asked, "Are you enjoying the camp so far?"

"If it weren't for my grandson I'd be sitting on my boat right now," he said with a smile.

"Ah, only a couple more days left," I said reassuringly.

He nodded and I said, "See you tomorrow", as I pushed open the locker room door, without giving the conversation a second thought.

The next day I noticed Bud standing in the same spot as I had seen him the day before, so I approached him.

"So, what do you say today?" I asked striking up a conversation.

"It's a great day for fishing! There's no wind. It would have been perfect!" He exclaimed.

"You like to fish?" I questioned.

"Hell no, but it keeps my wife quiet," he said with a devilish grin. I smiled back at him before stepping onto the ice.

The next morning when I got to the rink, all I could hear was laughter coming from the instructors' locker room. I entered slowly trying not to interrupt the discussion, and to my surprise, there was Bud holding court. He had the room in stitches as they left for the ice.

Bud and I remained in the locker room. "So you are going to join us today, eh?" I asked.

"Yeah, I'm helping out today because I owe Bob a favor," he said.

Bob was the camp director. Apparently one of the other instructors could not be at the session, so he asked Bud to help.

"I guess you and I will be working together." I said while leafing through the practice plan that was sitting on the bench.

"Well, I'm too old to be in charge, so it's your show, kid. I'll help you, but I don't want to be responsible for anything," he stated laying out the ground rules.

I opened the door for him to pass through to the ice as if to say 'no problem.'

Little did I know when we got on the ice, I was in for a surprise. It wasn't long after his first skate touched the ice Bud playfully knocked the stick out of the hands of the first player he skated by.

Then as that player was bending over to pick up his stick, Bud swept it down the ice.

And he said with a smirk, "You gotta get a better hold of that stick. Ya never know when something bad is going to happen!"

The surprised young boy looked up and smiled before chasing down his stick.

Then he skated by another player and then with a sarcastic tone asked, "Is that as fast as you can go?" The boy responded defiantly "No!" and took off with a burst of speed, determined to show Bud his very best.

After watching this, I was in shock. Complete disbelief!

Then I noticed the player whose stick Bud had knocked the stick out of his hand, sneak up behind him and gently tap Bud's stick with his to get his attention.

Bud growled, "You gotta swing harder than that kid to get the old boy."

The boy and Bud exchanged smiles and continued skating.

I started to watch Bud a little more closely, as he made his way around the ice, interacting with every player. In just a few minutes on the ice, Bud had all the kids smiling and every child had had a moment of his time.

The more I watched him interact with the kids, the clearer it was that these kids loved him. Bud knew exactly what he was doing. I knew right then that he was someone I needed to get to know: someone worth pursuing.

We worked well together during the classes. I set up and ran the drills. Bud would make his way around and talk individually to each of the players. He never pulled them out of the drill. He just quipped 'one-liners' or a few words of encouragement their way.

Every time the kids would smile or say something back to him, he loved it.

I had never seen anything like it.

I wanted him on the team. I had no idea what role he would fill, but the team needed to have him involved.

After the session, I thanked Bud for his effort and sincerely claimed, "You have a way with kids."

He smiled.

"I've never seen anybody interact with kids the way you did. They all love you," I said in admiration.

"Kids are easy and all they want is some of your time," he added.

"It seems like there is more to it than that," hoping he would elaborate.

"Listen, I've been teaching and coaching most of my life and I learned early on that when kids like you, you can teach them anything. If they don't like you, it doesn't matter what you know, you'll never get your message across.

The more you work with kids, the easier it is to relate to them," he said sensing that I really wanted to know more.

"You definitely have a gift with kids," I complimented.

"No, I wouldn't call it a gift; I just have fun when I'm out there and the kids seem to respond."

I knew there was more of a method to this than he was sharing, so I asked him if he would be out again the next day.

"Yeah, I'll be around. As much as I try, I can't stay away from the rink," he said.

All night all I could think about was Bud and every time I thought about him, I remembered what John said about coaching players today:

1. Kids play for coaches they like and respond to a personalized experience.
2. As coaches we have to sell the game to the kids, make it fun or they will not stay in the game.
3. As coaches we must tell them why, make them understand the purpose of what you are doing.

When I thought back on my day with Bud I realized that he had accomplished all three in the first few minutes he was on the ice. He was the epitome of what John wanted as a coach.

I had to have Bud involved with our team. I just knew it would be great for the kids, but I also knew that I would be in for an education.

I spent the rest of the night trying to figure the best or most effective way to approach Bud. I needed a 'sure fire' way that would engage this great coach. The invitation must be sincere, yet powerful enough to strike a 'coaching cord' with this man. I could see he loved the kids and he loved the game. At times he was aloof. And he did project an image of quiet resolve. But there was something else. In his eyes I could see something. My mind wouldn't let go of the dynamic image of Bud working with those young players. Behind Bud's apparent 'off-ice front' for disinterest I could sense something else. If I approached him the right way, he could come around.

The next day was the last day of the camp and I was anxious to get to the rink.

I saw him standing in his favorite spot in the corner where I had met him for the first time just a few days before.

I approached him and we started to talk. I commented on how much I had learned the day before. Then we started to talk about the camp and hockey in general, and I soon blurted out, "So what do you think about getting back into coaching."

"Coaching?" he said surprised. "I have no desire to coach. I have done my time. It's a young man's game now."

"No I don't mean coaching, I mean helping out," I said backpedaling slightly.

"Listen kid, I don't have the time. I'm too busy," he said trying to damper my enthusiasm.

"Bud, I really want to become a good coach for this team and I don't think trial and error is my best approach. I need someone who has been there to help me avoid the big mistakes that come from inexperience," I said.

"You have to make mistakes in order to learn. That's the most important part of the process," Bud said.

"I guess I'm intrigued by how you coach," I said, "I've been looking for coaching help for a while and have talked to quite a few people, but I haven't seen anyone or talked to anyone with your approach. I have tryouts coming up in a few weeks. I'd like to ask you if you would watch a couple of the skates with me," I said trying to find the scenario that would entice him in the door.

"Don't get me wrong; I miss working with kids. I get a kick out of it, but I am around the rink a lot with my grandson as well and I can't see me being able to commit to your team," Bud explained.

"I'm not sure I need you to commit to the team 100%. I would like to have you come out periodically during the year as a resource. In a couple weeks, I have tryouts, I would love to have you come out and watch a couple 'skates' with me. I'd be interested in hearing your thoughts or insights regarding the different players. Then maybe when the season starts maybe, you could join us for a couple practices and maybe a game or two to make sure the team is moving in the right direction," I explained.

"I don't mind helping you, but I'm not interested in being too involved or having too great of a responsibility when making critical decisions. That's your job!"

As we exchanged our contact numbers, I struggled to keep my composure. Part of me wanted to hug him, but I settled for a reserved smile. For the first time in the process, I had felt a sense of accomplishment.

The next task was finding a goalie coach.

With the number of goalies who missed having a goalie coach on the way up, you would think there would be a line a mile long of ex-goalies who wanted to give help to the next generation. Well, this was not the case at all. I don't know why, but it was nearly impossible to find someone who had played net and was willing to get involved.

What I decided to do was go to some local goalie clinics, camps and schools to see who I could find.

After going to a couple goalie clinics, I came across Tony, a young instructor at the camp, just twenty years old. He had recently played his last year of local junior hockey and the community college he was attending did not have a hockey team, so I figured he was perfect.

When I approached him, he was happy to get involved. After meeting Bud, I was on the lookout for a goalie coach who had an engaging personality, I liked that he was young and he still spoke the language of the kids we were going to coach.

I was excited to go to the next meeting as I felt I had recruited a great staff. I had three different generations of hockey covered and felt I had good diversity. I knew I had still had to work on Bud, but once he was re-connected with coaching I felt confident he would stick around.

COACHING CHALLENGE #5: STAFF RECRUITMENT

You can tell a lot about someone by the people with whom they surround themselves. Take a minute to answer the following questions to determine if you are being proactive in your approach to selecting your support staff.

1. How did you acquire your coaching staff for this season? Did you recruit them with a plan in mind, or did you just select from those who were around you at the time?
2. Who can you call to find out about good hockey coaches from the past?
3. Are there any summer leagues, tournament teams or hockey instructional camps where you could volunteer to expose yourself to different people?
4. Are there any young people you know that would love nothing better than to hang around a hockey team and learn to coach? Recently graduated junior hockey players, midget hockey players or university hockey players who are now working in the area and are out of hockey are great targets.
5. What approach do you need to take to get one of these people interested in helping out with your team?

6

PREPARING FOR TEAM TRYOUTS

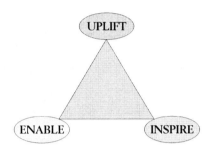

STRATEGY #6: PLAYER EVALUATION PLAN

Having a clear evaluation plan will create order and purpose to your tryouts. Order and purpose provide the opportunity to properly evaluate and ultimately select.

I DECIDED TO invite Bud and Tony for a barbecue in order to start planning for tryouts. The barbecue marked the beginning of the season for our team and I was hopeful that Bud would join Tony and I on the coaching staff full-time. Having him involved from the very beginning was important and I couldn't wait to hear his thoughts on tryouts.

I opened the discussion explaining how I thought we should run some development type drills so all the kids would come away with something from the experience and then have some evaluation scrimmages.

Bud interjected, "Tryouts are for evaluating and selection; wait for the season to start before you get too ambitious with running drills. Who knows we may have sixty kids or more trying out, it will be tough to see anything in a drill format."

"Start with a little goalie warm-up to start, and then run 5 on 5, 4 on 4 and

3 on 3 type scrimmages to give us a good opportunity to evaluate the kids' play," he continued.

Tony, looking at it from the goalies' perspective, liked the idea of running some drills, but goalie specific drills. He suggested that many times during try-outs it is tough to evaluate the skills of the goalies if we limited our view of them in warm-up type drills and scrimmages. This is especially true if there are 8 to 10 goalies.

"What chance are we giving the goalie that does not face any real shots during his scrimmage time?" he questioned.

Tony suggested that we take one of our four tryouts that we are required to give each player and bring extra nets on the ice, to run a goalie specific evaluation. After looking at it from many different angles and scenarios, we decided on our tryout plan.

TRYOUT 1:
- Ø Introduction and expectation meeting with the players
- Ø On-ice warm-up – 10 minutes
- Ø 5 on 5 scrimmage – remaining time

TRYOUT 2:
- Ø On-ice warm-up – 10 minutes
- Ø 5 on 5 scrimmage – 20 minutes
- Ø 3 on 3 scrimmage – 20 minutes

TRYOUT 3:
- Ø Goalie evaluation practice

TRYOUT 4:
- Ø On-ice warm-up – 10 minutes
- Ø 5 on 5 scrimmage – 20 minutes
- Ø 3 on 3 scrimmage – 20 minutes

EXHIBITION GAME #1:
Play a mixture of players who we have decided to be on the team and players who we have on the bubble.

EXHIBITION GAME #2:
Play our team (if decided at that point), or play a mixture similar to game 1.

We decided to invite the coaches from the 'A' and 'MD' teams (our affiliate or farm teams) to run the on-ice portion of the tryout. This way they could view and evaluate players who would be coming down to tryout for their team, and it would put our coaching staff in strictly a evaluation role for the four tryouts.

We also decided to video the scrimmages and the goalie specific portion of the tryouts to review; and make sure we were giving everyone a fair opportunity.

Finally, we engaged in a discussion on player selection. If two players were close to making the team and we had to decide which one would ultimately win the spot, what criteria would we use?

A week before tryouts, John invited us to the first of a series of coaching seminars. These seminars were for coaches to meet periodically over the course of the season and discuss our teams, our players and the latest training and development theory.

The topic of the first coaching seminar was what John termed "The Three Skill Speeds of Hockey." It was a simple way of looking at player evaluation and projection. Essentially, there are 3 skill speeds in the game of hockey:

SKILL SPEEDS OF HOCKEY

1. Skating speed – breakaway or separation speed, lateral speed, cornering speed, confined space agility
2. Hand speed or stick skill speed – shooting release speed, stick-handling range, quickness and elusiveness, one-touch passing
3. Read and react speed or hockey sense

All players' potential rests with the level of their weakest skill speed. When evaluating players, if you rate their skill speeds on a scale of 1-10 with 1 being the highest and 10 being the lowest, the skill speed that is weakest will be the level that represents their current ceiling or limitation.

For example, three players representing three different ceilings:

Skill Speed	Player 1	Player 2	Player 3
Skating	4	8	7
Stick Skill	8	3	7
Read and React	8	8	3

Player 1 has below average skating speed, but has excellent puck skills and hockey sense. In games where the pace of the game is very quick, Player 1 may have trouble getting to the spots on the ice to make his hockey sense and puck skill count.

Player 2 is a great skater and knows where to be on the ice, but is unable to handle the puck at the speed of his feet and mind. On a line with players who like to move the puck, Player 2 will struggle and commit unforced turnovers.

Player 3 is a very good skater, can handle the puck at his skating speed, but doesn't have a good sense of where to be on the ice. If your team uses a different system for each component of the game, or if your opponent forces you to make an in-game strategic adjustment, Player 3 will be indecisive and his feet will slow to the pace of his mind.

■　　■　　■

What we needed to decide was if two players were battling for one spot and each of them had different skill speed strengths, which skill speeds would we value most.

Our consensus was that we would select the player who had the best combination of skating speed and hockey sense (Player 2), and, therefore, their limitation or ceiling skill speed would be their stick skill speed.

We all agreed that our practices would feature skating development with a puck. Therefore, the players' stick skills would be the easiest to create big improvements in because of the amount of time the player would spend with a puck on our team.

The season officially started the first day of tryouts. We had fifty-nine skaters and eight goalies to evaluate for seventeen positions on our hockey team, and we had four practices and two exhibition games to make our final decision.

I was so excited at the season's first scrimmage that I was sitting in the stands half an hour before the kids even took to the ice. While I was waiting tucked away in the corner of the rink, with my notebook and line-ups ready, I killed the time by watching small groups of worried parents huddling together for comfort, while others were pacing quietly on their own. Having just come from the dressing room where I had welcomed the kids to the tryouts, I could not tell who were more nervous, the parents or the kids themselves.

The scrimmage got underway and Bud, Tony and I were able to get our first look at the players.

We had decided beforehand that during the tryout process that each of us would rate each player according to three groups:

1. Core Group – First, we wanted to identify a high performing group of players around which we expected to build the team.

2. Bubble Group – Secondly, we wanted to identify a group of players competing for a limited number of roster positions on the team.
3. Releases – A third group of players who were not ready to compete for roster spots for the upcoming season would also be identified.

After the first day, we met as a staff to compare our groupings. The easiest part of the discussion was determining the top end of the group or core players, and the bottom end of the group or the release players. The real discussion was the group in the middle. Each of us was going to have different reasons to advocate for different players. Our plan was to review our groupings after each skate to see if our lists had changed during the process.

Tony and I were both surprised when Bud asked for a schedule for the remaining tryouts. He had given us the impression that he was only coming to the first tryout. Clearly, he was starting to enjoy himself. Both Tony and I hoped it was a sign that he was looking to extend his commitment.

COACHING CHALLENGE #3: PLAYER EVALUATION AND SELECTION PLAN

1. Take a minute to select a player that you are familiar with and evaluate that player from the '3 Skill Speeds' assessment model. What skill speed do you feel presents the most opportunity to develop over the course of the season?
2. How do you decide between two players who have comparable personal skills but bring different strengths to the game?
3. What opportunity can you provide in your tryouts that give the goalies a chance to be evaluated according to goalie specific skills and movements?

7

TEAM TRYOUTS

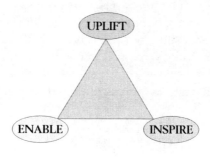

STRATEGY #7: CREATE EVALUATION SITUATIONS

For players who are on "the bubble" take the time to create situations in the tryouts to provide them the chance to play their way onto the team.

INVARIABLY, THERE ARE going to be personnel changes each year to keep up with the challenges that each level of competition presents. We had a chance to see all the returning players along with a few of the new impressive athletes. It was clear there were going to be 'broken hearts'. 'Cutting' or releasing players is the tough part of coaching, especially when dealing with twelve-year old children.

Our challenge was Kyle, a key offensive performer for this team in past seasons. He was a hard working player whose skating ability had finally caught up to him. He just didn't have the separation speed to elude checkers or the closing speed to make things happen on the fore-check; he was repeatedly knocked off the puck and you could see the frustration building. This happens to some players; they can become victims of early scoring success and if their skating is underdeveloped, the game can catch up to them. When the game gets faster and time and space shrinks, players like Kyle are unable to perform at the level they enjoyed in the past.

On the third day of the tryouts it was time for Tony to assert himself with the goaltender evaluation session. Tony was well prepared and Bud and I could tell that he was serious about his assignment. He held a pre-practice meeting with the rest of the on-ice help, and then went into the locker room to explain the purpose of the practice and the goalie evaluation drills.

Bud and I took a giant step back and allowed him to do his own thing. A few times, I wanted to jump in and help him out, but Bud caught me and was adamant that this was a great opportunity for us to see Tony's starting point as a coach.

Tony divided the ice into 4 stations with 2 goalies in each station. He had paired the goalies strategically, to create a competitive environment to evaluate his 4 early favorites to make the team.

- Station 1 focused on crease movement patterns that would challenge the goalies' skating ability in the crease.
- Station 2 was a recovery station to evaluate the goaltenders' ability to move, to make saves, recover and move to make the next stop. What I found interesting about this station was he started it off by forcing the goalie to get out of his net and stop a puck rimming around the end boards behind the net and then quickly recover to the front of the net for the first shot.
- Station 3 the goalies would face a sequence of breakaways. Each goalie would face 5 breakaways and then change; any more than 5 would turn a technique evaluation into a conditioning assessment.
- Station 4 was an athletic skill evaluation focused on rebound control. Tony was trying to see which goalies would challenge the initial shot with traffic in front, how they would maintain vision on the puck, control the rebound and scramble in the crease.

While Tony ran the on-ice session, Bud and I took the opportunity to pull kids aside for a chat. We had sent out a questionnaire with our letter of invitation for the kids a month before as a way to get to know them before they got to tryouts. Now we wanted to introduce ourselves to the kids and spend a little time with them. We managed to speak to all the players who we had identified as the core of our team as well as all the players on the bubble.

The most interesting conversation was the one we had with Brock. Our coaching staff had Brock rated high on the team from a skill perspective but we were concerned with a selfish and 'cocky' attitude he projected that seemed to stem from an inflated view of his capabilities. We were nervous about him because we questioned how good a teammate he would be.

When Bud and I pulled him aside to talk to him, we got a different perspective. We found him to be very competitive. We were surprised by the amount of pressure he put on himself to perform. The number of times he said 'I' in the conversation was alarming, but after meeting with Brock, we both felt his attitude was a way of protecting himself. He just appeared to be an arrogant kid. In retrospect, his behaviour was a coping method to hide his insecurities and the doubts that he had about his hockey ability. Our only concern after we spoke with him was how he would respond to coaching. We felt we could help Brock develop a more positive self-image with coaching and with a focused player development plan. Only with time could we really know what would work when we tried to coach him; we would have to wait to gauge his response.

After the first 4 tryouts we decided to invite twenty-four of the sixty-eight players to continue to the exhibition game phase of the selection process; 12 forwards, 8 defensemen, and 4 goalies.

I had been dying to get behind the bench to learn more about each of these players, but Bud convinced me again to step back. He felt it was important to continue to learn more about Tony's ability and give him an opportunity to be the coach to earn respect with the players.

Bud and I pulled Tony aside to tell him our plan for the game. When Tony heard that he was going to be the coach, we could tell he was nervous. Bud told him right away, "You have to be the coach Tony. At my age I'm apt to forget to change lines." Tony laughed and I could sense he felt better that Bud was going to help him. It killed me not to be on the bench but I understood what Bud wanted to do.

The hardest part of the exhibition games was deciding who was going to play, and what situations we could create for those players on the bubble to provide them with a chance for them to show us their best.

For example, our first concern was Kyle. We needed to put him on a line that would give him a chance to highlight his strengths. We decided to put him with two skilled players to see if he could recapture his finishing ability. Kyle played with Cain and Adam. Adam was a smart hockey player who saw the ice well and Cain was not only a great offensive player but also someone Kyle had played well with in the past.

As the game progressed, it became apparent that Kyle just was not going to make the team. His foot speed cost him a breakaway. Cain made a great pass to send him in all alone, but he got caught from behind and never got the shot off. His lack of speed also caused him to take a hooking penalty when a player pulled away from him. He had a couple good chances in the slot to shoot, but for the first one he was muscled off the puck and for the other he was boxed out easily on a rebound.

On the flip side, we were impressed with Robbie's play. We decided to play Robbie on a line with Forrest and Teddy. We felt Forrest would be a good fit because of his intelligent and hard working style. Teddy's size and robust style had a way of creating time and space. We felt this combination would help bring Robbie out of his shell.

This proved to be our best line of the night and one that I wanted to see more. Robbie showed flashes of being a quality player. He used his speed well on the fore-check and combined with Forrest he created turnover chances for Teddy in the slot.

The game ended in a 4-4 tie, but the result did not matter as much as the impressions we had formed of our players. One such impression that was hard to let go was the play of Carter. Carter was constantly up ice with the puck. Every time he got the puck in our end, he was looking to skate it. He was stripped twice for scoring chances and was caught out of position countless other times. We knew we had work to do to teach him to read his opportunities to lead the rush, or it was going to be a tough year for him.

Tony surprised me during the game; he was quite vocal on the bench and at one point was assessed a bench minor penalty for disputing a call. I called Bud on my way home to talk about it and he thought Tony's behaviour was likely because he was trying too hard to do well. Bud didn't think that it would be a problem, but suggested that we should mention the bench minor to Tony and gauge his reaction.

For the second exhibition game, we decided to coach our first game together. Before the game, Bud and I talked to Tony about the bench minor. Tony said that the emotion of the game sometimes swept him away, and he apologized.

The one player I decided to focus on was Brock. We were all interested in how he would respond to coaching so I decided to pose some questions to him after a couple of shifts to see how he would react.

I remember one instance in particular where he was on a two-on-one with Forrest and it was clear he had no intention of passing and he was going to shoot.

When they came off, I asked, "Hey Brock, on that last rush, did you see Forrest on the play?"

Immediately he defended his shot by saying, "No I didn't see him coach."

I asked Forrest, "Forrest, did you call for the puck or let Brock know you were with him?"

Forrest shook his head and replied, "No, I didn't call for it."

I then said, "Forrest you have to let Brock know you are with him; he could have really used you on that play as I thought you had the better shot opportunity."

Brock quickly jumped in saying, "Yeah Forrest, I didn't know you were there."

This approach was my way of telling Brock that I knew he had made a selfish play. I also wanted Forrest to know that he shares responsibility in the play as well. It taught both kids how important it was to communicate.

I couldn't wait for the next two-on-one that those two had; I wanted to see how both would react.

There were a couple of moments during the game when we could see Tony biting his tongue. He was a competitor and it didn't take much for him to get swept up in the emotion of the game. I was happy that he was able to hold his composure.

The following is the team roster and depth chart that we were able to identify following the tryout process.

TEAM ROSTER AND DEPTH CHART

FORWARDS

Teddy Big strong player whose offensive skill is untapped	**AJ** Gifted athlete, got all the tools, wonderful unassuming personality	**Cain** Small player, everyone questions his size and toughness, but has elite offensive skill
Forrest Average skills, very intelligent player who works hard, is a great teammate	**Adam** Raw talent, huge upside, gifted athlete, playing in AJ's shadow is great for him	**Zack** Lacks physical fitness so foot speed is a question mark, great ice vision and playmaking-ability
Robbie Tentative player, doesn't believe in himself, good skater, something about him shows potential	**Matt** Not a finisher, gritty player who skates well, may be a defenseman	**Brock** Selfish player who tends to think he is better than he is, works hard and has a very good skill set
Kyle Offensive leader in years gone by, small player with great heart and determination just not fast enough this year		

DEFENSE		GOALTENDERS
Sammy Good solid defenseman, does everything really well, nothing stands out as exceptional or poor	**Carter** Offensive defenseman, plays only when he has the puck	Ricky Small goalie, very quick, very aggressive and exciteable, loses his cool
Brownie Good defenseman, great foot speed, tons of heart, limited offensively	**Reese** Very small, quick and plays very tough	**Blake** Laid back goalie, tall, lacks foot speed, has solid positioning, very coachable
Bubba Big physical defenseman, foot speed is average but shows lots of potential	**Clifford** Bud's pick, below average puck skills but tough attitude, competitive and good skater	
Kelsey Big defenseman, good skater, doesn't use his size at all		

Developing this type of chart in your tryouts is a great tool to determine the type of team that you have in terms of strengths and early areas of opportunity.

The second exhibition game marked the end of the tryout process. The challenge became to tell unsuccessful players the truth in a way that was UPLIFTING, ENABLING, and INSPIRING to help them move forward. We decided to wait until the next practice before we let them go. There was no hurry to send them down to the affiliate, and releasing them after a game on the road might have made them feel as though that performance was the deciding factor. Besides, we felt it was important to take the time to speak to each of them individually.

After the game, we had our last coaches' meeting to reflect on the tryouts and to look ahead to the start of the season. As we were leaving Tony said, "Hey Bud, you're not leaving us now are you? You came with us this far, you have stay with us now."

Bud smiled.

"If you leave now, how could we not take it personally?" Tony said half joking.

"You guys don't need me," Bud said bashfully.

"Are you kidding?" I said. "We're a team now. You are part of us. I think I speak for the kids too, when I say we'd love you to stay with us."

"See, I knew this would happen," Bud said pausing. "All right, I'm in, but...!"

"I know, I know," Tony interrupted. "You don't want to have any responsibility or make any decisions. We got it covered," Tony said as the three of us broke into laughter.

There were some great moments in those six days that clearly defined the direction of the team, but probably none more important than the moment that Bud officially joined our staff.

From our perspective, the tryouts had concluded and the team had been decided.

COACHING CHALLENGE #7: PLAYER SELECTION PROCESS

1. What kind of situations can you create for players on your team to allow them to play themselves onto the team?
2. What evaluation process do you have that is goalie specific?
3. Create a "Team Depth Chart" with short player descriptions to help you determine the best situations to challenge your players.

8

The First Practice

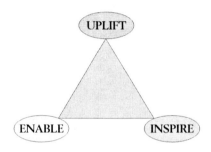

STRATEGY #8: ONE CHANCE TO MAKE A FIRST IMPRESSION

Plan and execute your first team practice to reflect the way you want your team to approach and perform during practice all season.

THERE WAS A nervous silence in the locker room just moments before our first practice and Bud could sense it. I could feel Bud's eyes on me as I studied my practice plan.

"Nervous?" he asked.

"Yeah, a little bit," I admitted raising my eyes to meet his.

"Well, if you aren't nervous, you don't care," Bud quipped. "You should be nervous; this is the most important practice of the year," Bud said capturing the importance of the laying the foundation of organization, discipline, execution, pace and intensity for the season in this next ninety minutes.

I thought the best way to set the tone would be with flow drills, including plays at the net for the goalies, and then move into some quick feet and agility with a puck drills; this would give Tony a chance to work with the goalies on his own. I was anxious to get into some small space one-on-one battles and then finish with a small space game. I constructed the first practice so I could emphasize that on our team, practice habits would reflect the habits we wanted to create for the games.

I was interested to see how hard these guys would push one another and eager to see how they would respond to a fast paced practice. I changed drills every 6 to 8 minutes to keep the drills fresh and the motivation high.

We gathered for short breaks between drills at the coaching board. Taking a minute between drills would establish routine and give me a chance to get the players used to reading the board. I am a big believer that teaching kids to read plays and positioning from the board is an important skill that would allow our team to make any necessary adjustments during the game.

I am sure we have all experienced how frustrating it is to try to point with our fingers to areas of the ice from the bench. We end up spending so much time trying to pinpoint the spot on the ice the message gets lost. I wanted all of our players to read a rink diagram because by taking a minute to draw drills from the board in practice, we would be able to use the same board to make in-game adjustments.

For discipline, I wanted the players on one knee any time I, or any other coach, was addressing the team. This position would ensure that I would have their attention and would be a valuable tool for teaching positioning.

There is nothing worse than whistling the play down to make position adjustments, only to have all the players continue skating. This technique would get them to stop on whistles and when they got a feel for when we wanted to speak, they would get on one knee automatically. Kids listen better when you limit their movement. Getting them on one knee is something I learned at the hockey school and I found it to be a great teaching tool.

Bud soon noticed something in the kids' practice habits that he knew would be his first teaching moment.

He had noticed when the kids missed a pass they would just pick up another loose puck and continue to the net. As soon as Bud saw it, he came right over to me and said, "Did you see that?"

I have to admit that I didn't really know what he meant because I thought the drill had great speed and pace.

After practice Bud exclaimed, "It drives me crazy when kids do that."

"Do what?" I asked curiously; I had no idea what had him so irate.

"When they just carry on after a missed pass and pick up another puck," Bud said.

Bud is a big believer that drills do not teach skills. People teach skills. A drill merely provides a repetitious opportunity to reinforce the habit the teacher is trying to create.

"This is what drives me nuts," Bud emphasized. "We spend all of our time looking for magical drills thinking if we had great drills we could teach great skills. It is a myth. The drill is only the vehicle that carries the message. The drill itself does not teach skills; people do," Bud said gaining our attention. "Instead of looking to steal drills one at a time, we need to spend more time creating drill runs."

"What is a drill run?" I interrupted.

"Drill runs are three or four progressive drills run in a sequence," Bud clarified.

"Let me ask you this," Bud continued. "How many times have you seen a coach run one drill for fifteen minutes?"

"I don't know. I suppose most coaches want to give their players time to learn the drill and give them enough repetitions to learn the skill," I answered.

"While that is a valid reason, what if I told you if you broke that drill down into 3 – 5 minute drills you would achieve much greater results?" Bud asked. Without waiting for my response, he continued. "As coaches, we have to make sure that each drill we have has a purpose, and that the skills we are teaching fall within a certain progression. I used to steal drills from coaches all the time, but the problem with that is where does the drill I stole fit in the development sequence? I cannot tell you the number of times I thought I found the perfect drill only to realize that my players were not capable of performing half of the fifty skills it contained. What is the point? What do we want to do; steal drills that look good or do we want to teach? If you want to teach, you have to find the beginning and build teaching progressions. A teaching progression is a three or four drill run. That is point number one!" Bud said.

"What is point number 2?" I asked sheepishly.

"I am glad you asked," Bud said with a smile. "Point number 2 is account-ability to purpose. You must know the teaching points of the skill and rein-force them with your players as they are performing the skill within the drill. I'll use that last drill you did as a prime example."

"If the point of the drill is to build good passing and pass receiving habits, and we as coaches allow these players to make bad passes and just continue with another puck, the drill is a waste of time. It becomes an exercise without value and I am too old to be out here wasting my time.

I loved to see Bud with this much passion for teaching. He was so into the practice it was awesome. I was looking forward to the next practice so I could see how he would address it.

Hearing Bud rant about purposeful drills made me self-conscious. I was the one out there trying to steal as many drills as I could, but after hearing Bud's thoughts my perspective was changing.

It made sense, we had to find ways to set up drills that provided quality repetitions for the players to learn the skill, and when it was running to hold the kids accountable to the teaching elements.

As first practices go, I felt that the practice flowed well. We were still carrying the extra players who we needed to release, but I felt the pace of the practice was good and the kids worked very hard.

Bud did his usual routine; by the end of the first five minutes, every player on the ice had felt his attention.

COACHING CHALLENGE #6: PRACTICE HABITS
Practice time is the best place to establish the foundation of your team.

1. What do you think Bud should do to create accountability in our team's passing habits in the next practice?
2. Name 3 practice habits that you feel are essential to the fabric of your team.
3. Take each of those habits you listed and illustrate how you are going to reinforce that habit inside of your daily practice habits.
4. Take your favorite drill and break it down into 3 drills.
5. Now take the drill and add another dimension to it to create a 4-drill sequence.

9

RELEASING PLAYERS

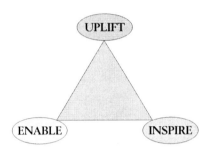

STRATEGY #9: SELECT YOUR TEAM AND CONTINUE TO INSPIRE THE DREAM

In the moment when a player is most disappointed lies an opportunity to uplift, enable and inspire. Don't miss it. It could be the only one you get!

"WHAT DOES 'AREA of opportunity' mean?" Bud asked while he was flipping through the player evaluations before practice.

"I think it sounds better than weakness, and it suggests possibility rather than limitation," I replied.

"I've never heard that before," Bud continued.

"Well, part of our purpose with these releases is to motivate these players to improve. By suggesting 'areas of opportunity' as opposed to 'finding fault', we give ourselves a chance," I explained.

"I like it!" Bud said with a smile.

After practice we had our meetings set up, I decided to speak to the goalies first, followed by the skaters and finishing with Kyle.

The challenge in these meetings was to find a way to turn a tough situation into an opportunity to UPLIFT, ENABLE and INSPIRE. Any of these players could play for us at one point or another during the season and it was important that they felt welcome.

I invited each player and his parents to join our staff as well as our affiliate coach for the meeting. In each case I opened by thanking them for their effort during the tryouts. Then I gave them an evaluation of their play, with the positive first and then a few areas of opportunity that I felt were the reasons why they were not able to make the team. I wanted to be as honest and forthright as possible, making sure they understood their areas of strength and the areas they needed to work on.

I had called Coach Stone and asked him for some quick feet and agility drills the kids could do off-ice to improve their foot-speed, which I included in their evaluation package. I also gave our affiliate coach some drills that he could incorporate into his practices to help improve their skating speed.

I then spent a minute acknowledging the natural disappointment and hurt that they were feeling. I wanted to encourage them to use this experience to motivate themselves to work hard and improve their skills to compete for a spot on the team in the future.

I followed the evaluation with an open invitation to join in all of our team practices and dry-land training sessions that we had scheduled with our team. I added each of them to our team email list to make sure they were up-to-date on scheduling and alike. I then invited the affiliate coach to express his excitement of having them on his team. He reassured them that he would do his best to work with these players, and to incorporate the drills we had suggested into his practices, so they could earn their way back to our team.

The meetings went well and all of the players expressed an interest in continuing to come out to our practices which, given the circumstances, was encouraging.

Releasing players from any team is very tough but for three of the kids it was especially difficult because they had played on the team the year before. In Kyle's case, we were splitting best friends, since Cain made the team and he had not.

In each case, I was able to UPLIFT the players by highlighting their strengths and by conveying our genuine willingness to help with their development. I invited them to continue practicing and developing with our team, and the affiliate coach welcomed them enthusiastically to his team.

I ENABLED them by providing the opportunity to continue skating with the team as well as providing them with development material in the form of dry-land and on-ice drills to address their areas of opportunity.

Then I encouraged them to use the experience as motivation to work on their skill deficiencies.

There is no way to take away the sting and the hurt that the released players feel. However, you can INSPIRE the player to move forward.

If we fail to work with them and with the coaches who coach them, we run the risk of them not being exposed to the proper development and falling further away from the team. The best gift we can give our team for next year is another competitive try-out.

COACHING CHALLENGE #9: RELEASING PLAYERS

1. Do you share my belief that the responsibility to provide development direction to the players who narrowly miss making your team lies with you?
2. What are three ways that you can maintain the talent depth at your age group for the next year?
3. What are some other ways you can uplift, enable and inspire players who you release from your team to continue to pursue their dreams?
4. What resources do you have to provide direction for these players to develop the areas that prevented them from making the team?
5. What is your relationship with your affiliate team coach, and how can you work together to help the development of those players?

10

Pre-Season Team Building

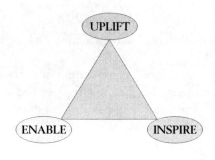

STRATEGY #10: BUILD A TEAM OR A CULTURE

Everybody's desire for acceptance and belonging creates the conditions for each of your players to bond as a team.

I HAVE TO admit that before my season plan meeting with John my ideas about team building included holding a pizza party and booking a sleep over tournament early in the season.

I had not been exposed to team building in my playing career in the sense that John described, so all this was new to me. On the heels of my meeting with John, I did a little research on the subject, and was surprised by the formal team building at the corporate level of business and even more surprised by the number of elite level (professional, national and college) hockey programs that have adopted this practice.

The biggest benefit that I found in the team building exercises I read was how the co-operative nature developed a feeling of belonging amongst the team members. When every player has a genuine belief in their role and feeling of belonging, their work ethic towards team objectives dramatically improves.

With each of these team building exercises, a different player would emerge to the forefront. It was amazing to see the different sides of the players' personalities reveal themselves as they became more and more comfortable with each other.

Bud was a big advocate of team unity, although his frame of reference was a little "old school." He said, "I like a team that behaves more like a motorcycle gang than a hockey team." He was suggesting that the best teams have a "mess with one of us, and you mess with all of us attitude." When I shared my team building plans with him, he laughed and said, "In my day if the coach wanted us to bond he would send us out to steal a car together, or start a bench clearing brawl to bring the team closer. Thankfully, times have changed."

My team-building plan started with an exercise designed to include the players in developing the operating framework of the team, the goal setting, code of conduct, consequences for inappropriate actions, communication guidelines, etc.

I wasn't a hundred percent sure what I was doing, but I thought I would jump into it with both feet and see where it would take us.

I brought the kids up to our hockey boardroom and started by dividing the team into three groups of four and one group of five. I then asked them to draw an open hand (marking five fingers) on a piece of paper.

I then directed the group to put the following heading on each of the fingers:

1. Team Goals – the objectives of the team
2. Team Rules – respect guidelines
3. Support – ways which we could support each other
4. Challenges – obstacles we expect to overcome
5. Habits – consistent behaviors that will lead to success

I then asked them to identify among their mini-groups five points for each heading and after a few minutes we compared answers to determine the top five for each.

The most interesting answers were the team rules. It shocked me to see the rules they wanted to implement. These kids were so strict that Bud and I joked that it might be easier to follow the rules in the military than on this team. It was funny to hear them talk about being on time and being respectful to the coaches. The most interesting rule they came up with was in regards to the team jersey. They viewed a team jersey on the floor as a sign of disrespect, so they made a rule that jerseys were to be on a hanger with the team logo facing out.

Once we had the framework complete, we made a master copy and I asked the group how we could keep this fresh in our minds and use the hand drawing as a constant reminder of what was important to us as a team.

They suggested that we laminate it and have the captain post it in the dressing room of each rink we played in before the game. I thought that was a great idea.

I then finished the team building session that day with a "Fact Sheet Exercise." This common exercise is used in many team-building situations and I thought it would be a nice ending to our session.

Players write an obscure non-hockey related fact about themselves that nobody else would know. Then we gather the facts and try to match the fact with the person.

It was comical to hear some of the facts. One player was fired from a paper route job, another played the harmonica, and the best one was a player who won a gymnastic competition when he was younger.

It proved to be a fun exercise with lots of laughter. You could really see the personalities of the kids come to the forefront; I felt like we were off to a good start.

COACHING CHALLENGE #10: TEAM BUILDING

1. What team building exercises do you know that could help pull the team together before the season starts?
2. What are some other ideas that you may have to give your team a bonding experience?
3. How can you provide opportunities for your players to be involved in the planning and structure of the team?

11

Fitness and Skill Testing

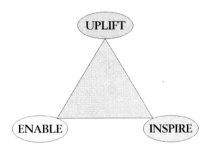

STRATEGY #11: SET TANGIBLE INDIVIDUAL AND TEAM GOALS

Create a system to measure development and provide an opportunity for your players to achieve success on multiple levels.

I LOOKED FORWARD to our road games. Bud and I traveled together. Each trip featured a different discussion about life, hockey and teaching. On our very first trip for a pre-season game, I asked Bud his thoughts on fitness.

"I just want the kids to be able to play at the level of their ability. I believe most players have such poor conditioning that they are unable to perform to their capability. Think about how many kids take shifts off, skirt their defensive responsibilities or pace themselves through a game and never display their true ability. I'd be happy just to see the kids be able to do what they *can* do consistently, let alone do something above their capability," Bud said.

Our discussion that day motivated me to call Coach Stone on the importance of Team Fitness and Skill Testing for minor hockey players.

I was fortunate to have been involved in Coach Stone's university hockey program because while I was at school he was just stumbling on testing and was using our team at the time as a study to explore it further.

Most hockey programs in university have someone using the team for their thesis. What started out as physical education or kinesiology students using our team as guinea pigs for their science experiments, expanded quickly when Coach Stone viewed the results.

As players, none of us had experienced testing of any sort before so we just assumed our participation was more for the benefit of the study, than for us.

After viewing the initial results from the fitness testing, Coach Stone began to research specific hockey testing and began to incorporate them into his season plan. He then used the results to motivate the players to work hard to improve the team's fitness and skills.

"There is something motivating and all-consuming about a tangible goal. When you are racing against the clock or reaching for distance, improvement becomes addictive," Coach Stone explained.

I really wanted to create a testing and development program that would accurately portray a player's fitness relative to the demands of hockey. How do you know if your players are in good shape? Coach Stone says from a conditioning perspective it is all about a player's ability to recover. In hockey, a player has to skate in quick bursts repeatedly in a forty-five second to a minute period. Then for our team, rest for 2 minutes or less and then repeat that process multiple times during the game. If a player gives his best effort during those first forty-five seconds, can he recover in the next 2 minutes of rest to give a similar effort in the next forty-five seconds? If he can, how many intervals or times can he repeat this process before he starts to pace himself or take shifts off?

We play 3 fifteen minute periods, and each player could expect to play as many as fifteen or eighteen shifts during the game. Therefore optimum recovery conditioning would be fifteen to eighteen intervals. If a player could give his best effort during a forty-five second shift, rest for 2 minutes, repeat that process fifteen to eighteen times, and see minimal drop off in performance, he is in game shape.

"Testing is an underutilized platform that has the potential to motivate your athletes beyond belief," Coach Stone said. "There are many benefits to testing your players but the four main ones should not be ignored.

1. It expands the levels of success a player can achieve; without specific measurable goals, your players and parents' only measure of success is wins and losses.
2. It is an opportunity to prove development; the first testing results establish a baseline for each player. Coupled with the season ending results, you can accurately gauge improvement.
3. There is accountability when the goal setting is personal and develop-

ment is in the player's control

4. There is relationship building when the coach, the player and his parents review the data together and form a partnership to provide the conditions of achievement.

I do not know how coaches, and associations for that matter, can afford not to include testing in their programs," Coach Stone said emphatically.

I was preparing for the start of our coach/family meetings, but after speaking with Coach Stone, I decided to wait until after we conducted the testing. After listening to Coach Stone, I could see that the testing was bound to reveal something that would provide me an opportunity to UPLIFT, ENABLE and INSPIRE each of our players.

Clearly, conditioning is a big part of helping kids play to their potential. Coach Stone gave me some great ideas on testing and the three tests that stuck out for me were as follows:

1. An on and off ice recovery test
2. An on and off ice agility test
3. A core strength test

I loved the idea of matching on and off ice tests because I wanted the kids to be able to have a way of gauging their off-ice workout progress. By having an off-ice test that could reflect their conditioning, the kids would be able to test themselves as often as they liked and chart their improvement.

I felt that if the testing portion was set up properly, the kids would find motivation to work hard away from the rink. My goal was to use the test scores to illustrate to the players that if they worked hard off-ice on specific aspects of their game, that improvement would carry over in their on-ice performance.

We executed the tests and they revealed some unexpected results.

For example:

Ø Robbie is a player who on the ice shows very little confidence with the puck, he is always looking to pass and rarely challenges players one-on-one, yet he recorded the top time in the skating agility with a puck test. In showing Robbie his test scores and game tape that shows his lack of confidence with the puck, we may be able to help him transfer his skills in to game performance.

Ø Zack's recovery was predictably the weakest on the team, but what was interesting was Brock had the second worst. Brock is a player who is always looking for opportunities to stretch his shifts out, but his recovery is poor. For Zack, we can help pinpoint fitness exercises to address his recovery. For Brock, we can use his test scores and game video to show how his recovery prevents him from showing his best consistently. We can then structure some fitness exercises to help him improve.

Ø Carter was a player who looks for every opportunity to skate with a puck during the game, yet finished in the bottom third in the skating agility with a puck test. This is another example of how the testing results would help us challenge and redirect the player towards more success.

The tests also confirmed a few predictions. For example, the players I considered the top athletes AJ, Sammy, Cain and Brownie, all finished in the top 10 in every test. AJ was the player who posted the fastest lap time and he also posted the top standing long-jump score. Clearly, there is a relationship between explosive power off the ice and speed on the ice.

There were also a few 'red flags,' for example, Teddy, Adam and Bubba all posted very poor core strength scores. These are all big physical players and to post such poor core strength scores is a potential injury concern.

The other 'red flag' was not relative to any player's shortcomings, but rather based on the testing results, we realized we had a problem. AJ posted the top score in each of the testing categories except for 1, where he finished second. The problem with his great test scores was how do we motivate and challenge a player who is setting the bar for our entire team? We knew that we were going to have to ask for the testing data from the next age group up to provide him with his goal-setting chart. Heading into our coach/family meetings, we did not have testing projection numbers for him.

I immediately called John to ask for those numbers. When I called him, he suggested that we take it a step further. He suggested that we work with that coach to get AJ out to some practices with that level to help challenge and motivate him.

COACHING CHALLENGE #11: TEAM TESTING

Incorporating fitness and skill tests in your season is a way of expanding your players and parents view success.

If you don't have a tangible improvement structure to track progress, the only measure of success available is wins and losses.

To allow your players to believe that the scoreboard is the only measure of success is very limiting and can be very discouraging.

By incorporating another standard to which players can evaluate their success expands the quality of their experience and gives them an aspect of their development that they can control. It is critical that we provide players with something that they can control that directly affects their development.

1. What other structures are in place on your team that expands the way you measure success?
2. What kind of tangible success measures can you record that would motivate your players to work on their game away from the rink?
3. What resources, development material or opportunity can you provide your players that will guide them to improving their scores?
4. How can you incorporate development into your season that will help them improve their scores?

12

Player/Parent Meetings

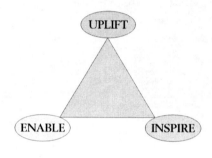

STRATEGY #12: CREATE A STARTING POINT

Create ground zero, design an improvement plan and involve the family in the program. This sets a natural improvement chart that motivates all to stay the course.

IT IS NO secret that most players hear some sort of coaching or instruction by well-intentioned parents on the way to the rink. I remember the confusion I experienced as a young player when my dad was teaching me to do one thing while my coach was instructing me to do the opposite. I remember wondering whose direction I should follow, and debating who I should disappoint with my choice. My father, who would ask me a million questions when I got into the car, or my coach, who would think I was purposely disobeying him. Choosing between the two was certainly not an enviable position. I wondered for years why each was speaking a different language when both professed to have my best interest at heart. I mean, honestly, how could it be in my best interest to be trying to do two different things at once?

I brought the topic of parent involvement in conversation with both John and Coach Stone, as I was interested in their respective thoughts. I wanted to see if there was any way to bridge the gap between coach and parent.

Interestingly, both felt that if our coaching staff were to maximize each player's development, we would need the parents as advocates to our program. Certainly, that was one of those things that would be easier said than done.

After a spirited discussion, we decided on the following as our parent involvement plan.

In school, there are regularly scheduled parent/teacher meetings to discuss the current position and progress of the child. In most cases, both parties are eager to forge a partnership in the interest of improving the education of the child.

In order to achieve a parent/coach partnership in hockey, it was clear we needed to find a way to involve the parent in the development process, without compromising our position. We certainly didn't want any parent to think that we were going to allow them to run their personal agenda through our team. We had a responsibility to each of the players on the team and we had to protect that. We weren't looking for approval from the parent in so much as we wanted to communicate our plan and invite support. How much easier would it be on the player and the development of the team to have the parent reinforcing the same ideas that the coach was presenting? We are in the business of developing people, collaborating with the most important influence in their lives would be critical.

There are three stakeholders in the growth of any player: the player himself, the parents who want the best for their child, and the coach who is trying to improve all the players on his team. It makes sense that the degree of cohesion between each of these entities would mirror the degree of success a team would have.

We decided the best way to achieve this partnership would be to establish a personal development program for each player, that if achieved, would not only make the players better, but also increase their capacity to contribute to our team's success.

The purpose of the family/coach meeting would be to establish a development starting point for the season, set a series of improvement goals for the player to work towards and have a way to measure progress.

The important aspect in goal setting is to continue to develop the players' strengths, while also addressing their areas of opportunity. Our purpose was to work with each family to illustrate the areas where we could create tangible improvement markers, such as time and distance type testing, as well as game performance numbers that we could track for each player. For example, we would track chances to score, net drives, finished checks, pass versus turn-over ratio, etc. We used the game film on the exhibition games and the testing results to determine a starting number.

We didn't need a statistician per se to track the numbers for each member of the team because the performance categories were different for each player. We were trying to create personal bests, so we created a player profile and tangible evaluation points that would reflect outstanding performance for that individual player. I felt we could enlist the parents' help with the recording process because the comparison was strictly personal and therefore created no need for well-intentioned parents to fudge or embellish the numbers.

By structuring it this way, we could have one family whose son played his best when he was physically involved in the game. They could track the performance of their son by recording the number of times he finished his check, he drove the net without the puck, and the number of turnovers he created versus committed, because those were the key areas of performance for that player. Then we could have another family track whose son was a playmaking forward whose game performance relied on the decisions he made with the puck. They could track the performance of their son by recording the total number of times he touched the puck, the number of successful passes versus missed passes, and the number of scoring chances he created.

By sharing with the parents that we did not intend to compare their son's game performance numbers to other players on the team, we could assure a greater level of accuracy.

After completing the team testing our coaching staff met to formulate a development plan for each player including his measurement profile. The plan laid out was similar to a scouting report starting with an overall description of the player, listing strengths, areas of opportunity and a plan for projection. After compiling the plan, we scheduled the family/coach meetings.

Our hope was by illustrating a genuine development plan for each player, the parent would feel compelled to collaborate with us to maximize the growth the plan could yield. If we were able to blend each player's development plan with the overall direction of the team, we would have a win-win situation.

So many coaches battle with the parents all season long. Many times because most parents view the game only from their child's perspective and the coach fails to show a genuine interest or concern for the development of that individual child. Trust is invariably broken, and the two sides compete against each other, tugging the child in opposite directions.

The family/coach meetings are a great way to open the communication lines, encourage the parents to participate in a coach directed initiative that benefit both the team and the player.

The hardest part would be to redefine success for everyone involved with the team. Our philosophy was that all players must improve for the team to be successful. Therefore, the emphasis must be on player development. The key to linking team performance to player development is to point out the development benchmarks that define our season to the parents. If the parents can recognize the development process they will support it, and we will have everyone on the team moving in the same direction.

The parent meetings were very interesting, and a few noteworthy revelations occurred that really made the process worthwhile.

Take Zack for example, it turns out in the off-season his parents bought him a gym membership to help his physical fitness. They became frustrated because neither Zack nor anyone else at the gym seemed to have a grasp on what would be important in a hockey-specific training routine, so eventually he had no program at all. Through the University team and Coach Stone I had access to all of that information and was able to get Zack on a hockey-specific strength and conditioning program.

Then there was Ricky, whose parents were very interested in the opportunity to discuss goaltending with Tony. Apparently, Ricky had a goalie coach in the past who tried to change his style and Ricky was apprehensive about goaltending instruction. Tony was able to articulate where he felt Ricky had an opportunity to improve his game and what kinds of things they could work on that would accomplish those things without changing his style. Tony wanted Ricky to know that his role as his coach was to build his skill base and emphasize his strengths.

One of the biggest challenges came from Brock's family meeting. It did not take long for us to realize where Brock's cocky attitude and overestimation of his ability had originated. It became obvious that Brock's family took the game and his performance very seriously and subsequently, Brock was under considerable pressure from home to excel. It was going to be a very delicate situation to try to turn their caring and passion for Brock into positive support instead of pressure.

The big surprise came when we met with AJ's family. His dad never played hockey; his mother doesn't come from an athletic background either. They knew AJ was a good hockey player, but they had no idea how good he was or what his potential might be. All they knew was that AJ loved the game and because of his activity in the sport, they became fans. They had to be the most unassuming family I had ever met in hockey; it was very unusual given his tremendous success to this point.

Those are just a few examples of how much we learned from each family and their approach to the game. The family/coach meetings were very enlightening given how differently each family approached the game. Bud remarked that he had been around the game his whole life and never experienced a process quite like it. I felt reassured that we had broken down quite a few walls in those meetings and if it made a difference for just one child, it was well worth the time.

COACHING CHALLENGE #12: FAMILY MEETINGS
Holding family development meetings is a time consuming process, but the benefits are immeasurable.

1. What other benefits do you anticipate from holding family/coach meetings with your team?
2. How important do you think it is for a player to know exactly how you evaluate him as a player, and what potential for development you believe he has?
3. Is there a way for you to set up your team's goal setting that creates accountability from the player in terms of effort, commitment and attention?

13

ENCOURAGE PERFECTION, PRAISE EXCELLENCE

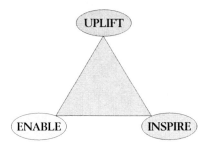

STRATEGY #13: ENCOURAGE PERFECTION, PRAISE EXCELLENCE

Where kids are concerned, you get what you ask for and your team will play the way you practice, therefore demand and praise quality practice habits.

WE WERE HALFWAY through the first of three practices we had before our season-opening game, when Bud's opportunity to create a teachable moment had come.

We had set up an assembly line drill. An assembly line drill is generally a timing drill (skate, pass and shoot type of drill) which is continuous. After the puck carrier takes his shot, instead of rejoining the line, he becomes responsible for starting the play the other way with the first pass. These types of drills are excellent because as many as half the team is involved in the drill at any given time. I typically use assembly line drills for a practice warm-up because of many repetitions in a short time period.

Perhaps the best part of an assembly line drill is its way of highlighting how important the first pass is to every play, whether it is in a practice or a game. If we miss the first pass, it compromises the overall timing and execution of the drill, which certainly parallels the demands of a game.

It wasn't long after the drill started when Bud noticed that when the first pass, or any other pass for that matter, was missed the intended receiver would look for another loose puck in his pattern and scoop it up to make the next play.

If the drill is designed to finish with a shot, you can bet that all players will look for an opportunity to shoot, and if the puck they are supposed to receive does not arrive, they will find another one. This was Bud's pet peeve and he was not going to let it go much longer.

He watched this scenario play out three or four times before asking me to stop the drill. Tony and I watched as Bud skated purposely to center ice to address the group.

"So Matt," he began, "how many pucks are on the ice in a game?"

"One," Matt replied quickly.

Bud paused and then spotted Forrest. "Forrest, how many pucks are on the ice in a game?"

Forrest replied emphatically, "One!"

Bud paused again, while everyone anticipated a punch line coming.

Now diverting his attention toward Sammy, "Ok, Sammy, do we play the way we practice?" Bud asked changing his line of questioning to lead them into his teachable moment.

"Yes Bud," Sammy replied.

Seemingly waiting for the right moment, and hoping to have grabbed the collective attention of the team, he then offered the following:

"Well help me out then, if you are saying that there is only one puck on the ice during a game, and you all believe that we play how we practice, then why when a pass is missed do you just pick up another one?" Bud said before pausing again to let the question sink in.

"If there is only one puck in a game, and we want to treat each practice as though we are preparing for a game, then we have to play one puck in practice. That means if you miss a pass, you have to chase it down and play it as though it is the only puck on the ice. I hope that will put some pressure on the passer to focus on making a quality pass," Bud finished, then turned to me with a wink to signal me to restart the drill.

Predictably, the kids were over-cautious with their passing. The speed of the drill dropped significantly as the players made a greater effort to complete passes, but a worthwhile investment in creating a new practice standard.

Bud's teaching moment was the first time he had really asserted himself to the kids. Tony and I noticed the impact immediately. We both watched Bud jump into the practice encouraging each player to concentrate on their passes, urging them to take pride in what they were doing. I joined in and then Tony did as well, and we watched the pace of the practice gradually pick up more speed.

There aren't many coaches who wouldn't like to dramatically increase their teams' ability to move the puck in chains of successful passes. The most difficult aspect of the game to teach is teammates interacting with one another offensively. I believe Bud changed the way our team moved the puck with that one teaching moment. He changed the attitude and established a standard of quality that we were to expect from our players at all practices.

When practice ended, we assembled as a staff for what had become our custom. I asked Bud to expand on his practice passing theory for Tony and me.

He responded by asking, "What is the consequence during a game when our team suffers on a missed pass?"

"A turnover," I replied.

He nodded and then asked, "Whose responsibility is it for a pass to be completed?"

"Both the passer and the pass receiver share the responsibility. The pass receiver has to present himself for a pass in open ice, and the passer must deliver the puck to the right area at the right time," I responded confidently.

"Exactly", Bud said with his enthusiasm rising. "So what happens in practice?" He asked. "What reason would the pass receiver and the passer have to concentrate on executing a perfect pass, when the pass receiver is just going to puck up another puck if the pass goes astray?" Bud asked, gaining momentum.

"Well none, I guess," said Tony, not wanting to be left out of the discussion.

"If neither the passer, nor the pass receiver cares if the pass is completed, where is the development? Maybe a better question is: what possible chance does the pass have to be completed when both players are under pressure in a game, if they practice with the safety of picking up another puck?" He said finishing his point.

"So how do we hold them accountable?" I asked thinking ahead.

"We start by forcing them to play one puck for the duration of each repetition. If the repetition requires three successful passes before a shot, then all three passes have to be successful or there is no shot," Bud suggested.

"That means if a pass is missed during the sequence, the intended receiver must chase it down to wherever the puck lands on the ice before making the next play. Then we teach the next pass receiver to keep his feet moving and provide good support wherever the next pass is coming from, exactly what he would have to do in a game situation. What we are hoping for is that the kids begin to put pressure on themselves to make good passes. We have to make it cool to make good passes," Bud went on to explain.

"I can really see how something like this can take on a life of its own," I said with excitement.

"Great!" Bud said. "Now apply the same theory to shooting. When the drill you are using finishes with a play at the net, how do you instruct your players to shoot?"

"I don't know, shoot the puck on net, I guess," I said hoping he wasn't asking a trick question.

"Is that what you want?" Bud asked.

"What do you mean?" I asked.

"How many kids do you know shoot to score on every shot?" Bud asked continuing his point.

"Not nearly as many as I would like?" I said with a smile.

"Most players will give you only what you ask for. If you only ask for a shot on net, they are not likely to go the extra step and truly aim for open net," Bud explained.

"The two things you hear coaches consistently complain about in games is their teams' inability to pass the puck and finish plays at the net," Bud said. "If you don't ask your players to concentrate on creating good passes and shoot with a purpose in practice and hold them accountable, it is impossible to expect them to do it under the pressures of competition," Bud said smiling.

Bud's passing and shooting theory stuck in my mind for a few days. I reflected on the teams I had played for and the way we moved the puck and finished plays. I had never heard of this approach. I can remember coaches that I had played for penalizing us for missing the net in shooting drills with push-ups or alike. Thinking about that approach now, I remember as a player just throwing the puck at the net, to make sure I didn't have to do the push-ups. Was I training to use my shot to try to score, or was I training just to lay the puck on the net?

Over the two practices leading into our regular season opener, our new standard of passing became a theme and the kids had responded really well. I noticed the speed and pace of the drills getting back to where it was before we imposed the pressure to complete passes. It still wasn't where I wanted it to be but I was willing to allow time for the kids to adjust.

In speaking with Tony and Bud, one of the changes I had to make in my practice planning was to include the key teaching points of every drill, so each coach could reinforce the important areas of execution in each drill. Tony had mentioned that in some of the drills, he wasn't sure which part of the drill needed the most emphasis. With that in mind, I wrote the key teaching points in red ink on the practice plan for the remainder of the season.

COACHING CHALLENGE #13: SHAPING PRACTICE HABITS

1. Identify three practice habits that your team has that you know, if you allow to continue, will surface in competition.
2. Take each of those practice habits and create a teachable moment. How can you use questioning to lead your players to realize that these habits need to change?
3. Then take each of those practice habits and create a measure of accountability or a rule that forces your players to make the adjustment.

14

ROLE MODEL

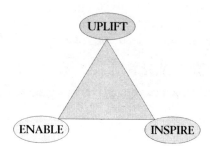

STRATEGY #14: BE YOUR TEAM'S ROLE MODEL OF CLASS AND RESPECT.

You will only get respect if you are willing to give it.

IT WAS ONLY the third game of the season, but Bud and I knew we had a problem.

Bud turned to me on the bench and asked me "Is there a backdoor in the arena? I am embarrassed."

I knew exactly how he felt as we both stood in shock and disbelief as we watched Tony come completely unglued. His aggressive approach to the officials earned him a well-deserved game ejection.

Bud and I had already pulled Tony aside after the first exhibition game when he earned the team a bench minor for expressing his disagreement with a call by the referee. That penalty put our team two men short late in the third period, which led to the game-tying goal on the ensuing 5 on 3 power play.

Tony fully deserved the penalty, but his conduct really was not my style. I have yet to see a referee change his mind on a call and until I see that happen, I believe that our interaction with the referee should be in an effort to get the next call. Moreover, the pressing issue was the example Tony was setting for our players.

In the first game of the season, Tony took another bench minor. He was apologetic realizing that his penalty had cost our team a win in the first game. He tried to rationalize his behavior by expressing his frustration with what he termed 'incompetence' on the part of the referee.

Bud tried to stress our point of view by saying, "It really doesn't matter how competent the refereeing is in a game, if the kids see you berating a referee, they will follow your lead. We are setting a bad example right now and I am not comfortable with that."

He went on to say, "When you debate every call the way you are right now, you are building excuses for your players. We don't want our players to look for any excuses for why they lost a game; we want to teach them to focus on things that they can control, like their own effort, their attention to detail, etc. Besides Tony, if I want to hear excuses, I'll listen to my wife!"

Tony had agreed with Bud and I, and we felt that we had addressed the problem. That is until the third game, when Tony lost control of his emotions and eventually earned an ejection from the game. I was embarrassed and was at a loss about what to do next.

After the game, Tony was still fuming. My embarrassment quickly turned towards anger towards Tony, so Bud suggested that we leave it for the night and have a meeting at practice the next day.

Bud must have recognized that I was still very upset, so he asked me to stop off at Tim Horton's for a quick bite before heading home.

I have to give Bud credit; he knew exactly what to do. Bud put the blame squarely on our shoulders for not making a greater impact on Tony after the first incident. He said that it is our problem to fix and that we needed to make certain that after the meeting the next day, Tony would have a clear understanding of not only our philosophy regarding referee interaction, but specifically how we wanted to conduct ourselves as a staff. Here is how we laid it out for Tony:

REFEREE INTERACTION PHILOSOPHY:

- In every game, there are three teams on the ice; our team, our opponent and the officials. While we don't need the officials to be on our side, we certainly do not want to give them any reason to work against us.

Our approach:
- Always work for the next call
  - o Instead of debating the call itself, try to make the official think about

his positioning to make the call in the first place. Many times when referees miss calls, it is due to their lack of positioning.

o Use line changes to build a rapport – the referee must look at your bench after every stoppage in play during a hockey game. Take this frequent communication opportunity and build a rapport. Never miss the chance to communicate with the referee directly during all line changes.

⊙ This constant non-threatening interaction with the referee gives him the impression that our bench is organized and our approach in this situation may make him feel comfortable to come to our bench to discuss situations, should they arise.

⊙ A simple head nod when we don't intend to change allows him to keep the game moving which he appreciates; we can also develop a signal for when we do want to make a change.

⊙ The goal of building a rapport through line changes is to open the lines of communication.

o When the linesman is on the blue-line closest to our bench, always talk positively about the calls he has made.

o When making an argument on a call, make sure you get down off the bench and speak to him at his level with a respectful tone.

▦   ▦   ▦

Most leagues have a core group of officials who are responsible for games at our level, so it is likely we will see them many times during the season. We want to conduct ourselves in a way that each referee crew will remember us as respectful and approachable.

After hearing our philosophy and specific examples of how we want to be-have in certain situations, Tony began to understand how important it was to build a positive relationship with the officials, and to use this relationship to set a good example for our team and maybe catch a break somewhere during the season.

We decided that it was the role of the head coach on our staff to be respon-sible for building a rapport and interacting with the referees, largely because the head coach would be the one interacting with them during line-changes. We felt having one person would help make our bench more approachable.

During the games that followed, Tony struggled with his emotions, but to his credit, he followed the plan. Bud remarked after our fifth game that he was proud of Tony for his control and reassured him that it would get easier with every game.

It was a good feeling to have succeeded in our first bout with adversity. Bud's experience came to the forefront during this process and while I didn't expect my first problem to come from my staff, ironically and fortunately, it had brought us closer together.

COACHING CHALLENGE #14: BUILDING RAPPORT WITH OFFICIALS

1. Take a minute to reflect on you recent coaching and think back to a time in which your reaction to the referee built an excuse for your players.
2. How many calls have you convinced the referee to change because of your ability to make an argument?
3. What can you do to improve your rapport with officials?
4. How do you think these new measures will affect the way your players react and respect the officials?
5. What can you do to create respect and accountability towards the officials within your team?

15

DEVELOP LEADERS

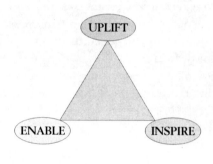

STRATEGY #15: DEVELOP LEADERS

While there can only be one captain on a hockey team, look for ways for all of your players to be in leadership positions at various points during the season.

WE HAD JUST finished our sixth game of the season and Bud and I could sense that the team was restless; we knew exactly what was on their minds . . . Who was going to be the captain?

We really had not made an effort to that point in the season to identify the leaders of the team, but we knew the time was approaching fast.

The easiest way to handle the situation would be to name AJ as the team's captain. After all, he had been the captain of the team the previous three years, and was by far the best player on the team. While AJ was a good leader by example, he was a reluctant leader. His personality was reserved and laid-back, he did not assert himself in leadership situations, he just wanted to play hockey.

After watching the team play the first six games, it was clear the team needed a new leader. While we had many skilled players, we didn't have a good team, in the true sense of the word. A change in the leadership of the team was one of the steps we felt would make a big difference in changing the culture of the team.

The big question was, if AJ was not going to be captain, how do we give it to someone else without making AJ feel that we didn't believe in him. Our goal was to lift the burden of being captain from AJ and teach him leadership skills and put him in leadership situations without the title. Besides, we knew there were other kids who were not only ready for the challenge, but would benefit greatly from the added responsibility. It was a delicate situation.

We decided it was best to pull AJ aside and talk to him about being captain and see what his thoughts were. I don't think any of us were prepared for AJ's candid response.

I opened by asking AJ who he thought the leader of our team was.

He said, "Honestly, I think Forrest is the leader of the team."

Naturally, I then asked him why.

He said, "I don't know; he just knows what to do and what to say. Everyone respects him and it seems when he talks everyone listens."

Then Bud interjected, "AJ, aren't you the leader of this team? I mean you have been captain for a few years now haven't you?"

"Yeah, I have been the captain, but I think Forrest is a better leader. I really don't know what I am supposed to do. I feel weird sometimes knowing I am supposed to say something, but not having a clue what I should say. I'd like to learn to be a better leader, but right now I just want to play," AJ said quietly lowering his head.

"We need a leader who can become an extension of the coaches and challenge guys to get better. Do you really think Forrest is that kind of guy?" Bud challenged.

"Absolutely!" AJ said looking up.

We were all surprised to hear this coming from AJ. When you watched him play, he looked like he was playing at a different speed than everyone else, but when we asked him about being the team captain he said he didn't know what he was doing. It was interesting to say the least.

Bud said to AJ, "I can't imagine what it's like to have everyone expecting a great thing from you every time you step on the ice, wearing the "C" probably doesn't do anything to take that pressure away, eh?"

AJ smiled knowingly.

Clearly, Bud connected with AJ, and we could see AJ started to relax. He knew Bud understood what it was like for him. Bud and I both felt AJ could be a great leader, but he needed time to learn how to be comfortable and effective in that role.

I said to AJ, "We think you could be a great leader, but you need time to grow and find comfort in that role. I think you should be a leader on the team, but not necessarily the captain just yet."

AJ nodded becoming more at ease in the conversation.

"I guess what we are worried about is that if you aren't the captain of the team that you will feel as though we don't believe in you, which couldn't be further from the truth," I said.

"I just don't think I should be the captain of this team. I think Forrest should be," AJ said assuring us to make a change.

While we weren't sure who was going to be captain, AJ made his first step to being a great leader that day.

After speaking with AJ, we talked as a staff about who we felt were the leaders of the team. I felt Sammy, Forrest, AJ, Bubba and Teddy represented the leadership core of the team. I didn't know who would be the captain, but that was my group to pick from.

Bud also liked Reese; he said that he showed leadership on the bench. Reese was always positive with the players and had a knack of speaking up at the right time.

Tony more or less agreed with us, although he thought Teddy had the most presence on the team outside of AJ.

When our staff meeting concluded, we decided to call John and Coach Stone to hear their thoughts about how we may determine which player was the true leader of our team. My first call was to John and he believed any team captain should be a reflection of the team identity.

"Every team has to have an identity, a style, a character. This identity reflects the characteristics that will make the team successful," John said.

He went on to say, "The strengths of the leader should mirror the identity of the team. As a coach, you have to determine the type of team you have, and then select your captain based on those criteria."

"For example, if you feel your team will be successful because they are relentless and tireless workers who constantly out-hustle their opponent, then your captain should be the best example of that," he continued.

While John said that teams take on the personality of its leaders, he also stressed there is no accountability like teammate accountability. If you have the right leader, he will create accountability through his example. Having a captain that reflects the team attitude and characteristics is a way of setting the bar for every other player on the team.

My next call was to Coach Stone.

Coach Stone took a very different approach to determining the leadership on a team. His approach was to stage an activity challenge, where the team would have to work together to complete the task. His goal was to set up the challenge, then stand back, and watch the leader emerge.

"You won't know who your leader is until a situation arises when leadership is needed to move ahead," Coach Stone said.

"The leader I want is the player who is going to plug into the situation and make good decisions in the face of adversity. Who wants a leader who is a great 'rah rah' guy before the game starts, but when things start going bad during the game, gets swept away with negative emotion?" He asked.

"To me, you need to find out who is going to organize the group in a positive way when they are in chaos. I stage one of these activities every year to help me determine who the leader is on my team," Coach Stone added.

He then went on to describe three of these activities.

ACTIVITY #1: OVER THE WALL

To set up the exercise, find two trees, posts or alike about 10-15 feet apart and suspend a rope eight feet off the ground between the two, to create an imaginary wall. Then get a 10-foot wood plank and gather the group on one side of the imaginary wall.

Instruct the group that they have 30 minutes to find a way to get the entire team over the wall using the wood plank as a tool if they so desired, then leave them to it.

Invariably, there is a part of the team that just wants to get started and try the first idea that pops in their head. Then there is another part of the group that is brainstorming all the reasons why the first idea won't work. After a while a group emerges that begins to brainstorm all the ways they could succeed in the task, decides on a course of action, sells the rest of the team on their idea, and then organizes them to execute the plan. The leader of that third group is the captain of your team," Coach Stone explained.

ACTIVITY #2: THROUGH THE HOLE

To set up the exercise, again find two trees, posts or alike about 10-15 feet apart. This time you need to construct a rope wall with nine, 2 foot by 2 foot squares. Then hang the rope wall so the bottom is about a foot off the ground.

Instruct the group that they have 30 minutes to find a way to get the entire team through one of those holes. The entire team has to go through one hole without touching one of the sides and without a break in the "team chain". Once either someone touches the sides of the hole or the team chain is broken that hole becomes closed for the remainder of the exercise, it is effectively eliminated as a passage; they have to start again using a different hole. Players must be touching each other continuously as they go through the hole to ensure continuous movement through the hole.

The exercise is complete when the entire team goes through one of the holes successfully, or they manage to eliminate all 9 passages.

"Again, there is always a group that wants to get started right away without thinking, and they manage to eliminate a couple passage ways right away. A second group waits for someone to come up with a good idea. Then there is a third group that tells the first group to stop closing holes and wait until they think it through and can come up with a plan. Then they think of all the ways they could do it, decide on a course of action, sell their plan to the team, and organize the group to execute the plan. The leader of that third group is the captain of your team," Coach Stone reiterated.

ACTIVITY #3: TEAM ON A BOX

This one is a great exercise for younger teams and allows you to see which kids are demonstrating leadership qualities.

To set up the exercise, bring in a milk crate and turn it upside down in the middle of the room.

Instruct the players that the goal is to get everyone on the milk crate at once. That means for a period of 5 or 10 seconds everyone has to be completely off the floor and on the milk crate.

The three groups will emerge and the group that takes a minute to think of the possibilities, formulate a plan, sell the plan, and then organize the execution of the plan is the team's leadership group.

Coach Stone went on to say, "You'll find the kids love doing the activities, they are wonderful team bonding exercises and the benefits of the exercise extend well beyond its original purpose. The other issue that is important to bear in mind is the importance of all players on your team to learn leadership skills.

You must develop a plan to create leadership opportunities for every player on your team. What can you do to create leadership opportunities for each player on your team?" Coach Stone challenged.

For the next half hour we bantered around many ideas, the following are a few that we liked the best:

LEADERSHIP ACTIVITIES INVOLVING EVERY TEAM MEMBER:

1. Start a "Guest Coach" program within the team. Divide the team into groups of three or four players. Each practice one of these groups is responsible for selecting/designing, presenting and teaching a drill for the team. This could be your warm-up drill for each practice.
2. Start a mentorship program with your association's tyke/timbit or learn to skate programs where you assign groups of your players to volunteer to help with the team.
3. Develop "Position Leaders" for each game (Forwards/Defense/Goalies). Position Leaders are responsible for motivating the players in their group for the game.

After thanking Coach Stone for his expertise, I took my notes from both John and Coach Stone and we tried to figure out how to take the best from each of their approaches and apply it to our team.

We decided that we loved Coach Stone's idea of staging a team building exercise; we were all trying to predict who would be in what group. We really liked Activity 2 because of the consequences of having the holes close if they didn't plan properly. That third group was likely to step forward pretty quick and we liked that.

We also liked John's idea of making sure the leadership was reflective of our team identity. The biggest issue that surrounded our team was that we still played an individualistic-style game. We really hadn't seen an identity with the team to that point, and there certainly wasn't any accountability from teammates through our first six games.

We took the next few minutes to talk about our team identity to see if we could determine the initial criteria.

Clearly, any team or individual who has experienced any success has a strong work ethic and our team was no different. Our talented players like AJ, Sammy, Cain and Adam each demonstrated a strong work ethic. As a team, we worked hard, just not together. We determined the following characteristics that we hoped would be the beginning of our team identity.

TEAM IDENTITY CHARACTERISTICS:

1. Unselfish
   * While we weren't selfish as a group, we were individual. The team got away with this in the past and now it had become part of their character. That individual mindset had to change.
2. Positive
   * We noticed that when we were behind in games, the bench went quiet. We really didn't have anyone who spoke up when the pressure was on. When we were winning games, our team was all smiles and giggly; the atmosphere was very different than when we were behind.
   * We would like our team to be more even keel and consistently positive regardless of the situation.

3. Tight
   * As with many teams we had some cliques we needed to break down, nothing that had presented a problem to that point, but we knew we had some new players that needed to feel part of the team. Bud also commented that he noticed the same kids sitting together in the dressing room.
   * The team wasn't one that has had to rely on each other very much to be successful. We wanted to be more of a unit in the face of challenges.

4. Disciplined
   * A big problem on the team was discipline. We wanted to foster a pack mentality. "If you challenge one of us, you have to take on all of us." We needed to develop a disciplined and team-oriented approach to physical challenges.

5. Determined
   * We felt we had players who showed mental toughness, but as a group, we lacked collective determination. We felt if we were to reinforce a team first attitude, we could achieve a sense of pride in our team and a collective determination to be successful.

■   ■   ■

If I had to pick one player who best exemplified these characteristics, I would pick Sammy.

Bud suggested that we needed a passage or a quote that would represent our team's identity, so we chose the popular Wolf pack passage.

"The strength of the pack is the wolf, and the strength of the wolf is the pack."

We felt that this passage would help the kids identify with the kind of team we were building.

We brought the kids into practice an hour earlier than usual to set up the team building activity. Tony built the rope wall the day before and had set it up outside between two trees. We took the kids outside to the activity and all of them wondered aloud what we were about to do.

Right away Forrest asked, "Hey Coach, what are we doing?"

"I brought my fishing net to see if I could catch a hockey player. God knows there isn't one here," Bud quipped.

"No seriously, what are we going to do?" Teddy persisted, eager to find the purpose.

Once everyone was together, I told the team this was a team building exercise that would be a fun challenge. I explained the objective and the rules and encouraged them to get started.

Bud had positioned himself right in front of the rope maze; I could tell he was anxious to close some holes.

Once the kids got started, Bubba, Brock, Cliff and Ricky went right to the wall and wanted to get going. Ricky, in an attempt to describe how he thought it should go, put his hand in the middle of the hole and then took it back out. Bud jumped up and quickly put a piece of tape on the hole, and announced Ricky had just eliminated the first hole.

The Teddy, Forrest, AJ, Sammy and Cain group was forming and they started brainstorming. Tony and I felt that this was our third group forming.

It wasn't long before Bubba and Brock were lifting Reese through another hole. Reese had made it successfully through the hole and now Bubba and Cliff were lifting Brody through. Everything was fine until they decided to put Zack through and he accidentally touched one of the sides to close off the second hole.

When Bud announced the closing of the second hole, Forrest ran over to tell Bubba to stop and wait until everyone was ready. They had already eliminated two of the nine holes and we weren't even five minutes into the exercise.

It was clear that Forrest was the leader of the third group and he began to take more control over that group. Sammy, AJ and Teddy were right in there making suggestions to help formulate the plan.

Once the plan was complete, they decided what order the group was going to go in. Interestingly, they decided that Reese, who was the smallest player on the team, should go last, and Cain the second smallest, should go second last, so he could lift him through.

Forrest, Teddy and AJ were right at the front of the maze, as they had taken control of the entire operation. Sammy was organizing the team to ensure everyone went in the proper order.

Five minutes later and some tense moments, they successfully completed the task.

What was amazing was how they reacted when Reese made it through without touching the ropes. It was as though they had just won the league championship and Reese had scored the winning goal. They mobbed him as they cheered wildly. You could see the sense of accomplishment beaming in the kids' faces.

They were still excited minutes later when Bubba asked, "Hey Coach, do you have any more of those, that was fun!"

Mission accomplished.

We brought the kids back to the locker room to get ready for practice and I decided that it was the perfect time to announce the leadership of the team. I told the kids to be ready five minutes before practice as I had a special announcement.

Tony and Bud stayed in the room to talk to the kids. The stories grew by the minute as they reflected on the exercise. They poked fun at each other and the atmosphere of the room was the best we had seen.

The positive energy, the great interaction and the laughter was fun.

Five minutes before practice, Bud, Tony and I addressed the group to announce the leadership.

I started by clarifying the purpose of the exercise we had just completed.

"I take it you guys liked that exercise we did outside?" I asked giving more life to the room.

"Yeah!" They shouted back in unison.

"Well that exercise had many different objectives. Clearly it was fun, and you can see how it has a way of pulling a group together, but most importantly, it gave us coaches a chance to see who the leaders of this team are. Bud, Tony and I were curious to see which of you would take charge, take the time to think of a plan, organize the plan and execute its completion. Who do you think took control and led you through the exercise?" I asked.

AJ was the first to speak up, "I thought Forrest was our leader."

You could see the group nodding their heads and Bubba started to clap his hands, leading to a round of applause.

"You know guys, we felt the same. We thought the group of Forrest, AJ, Sammy and Teddy took control and really led the team to accomplish the task," I continued.

"It is clear to us that Forrest has shown that he has the qualities needed to be captain of this team," I announced proudly.

"What do you think, is Forrest the captain of our team?" I asked to re-energize the room.

"Yeah!" They yelled collectively.

All the kids stood up and walked over to Forrest to shake his hand to congratulate him.

When all the kids sat back down, I proceeded to announce the remainder of the leadership group.

"The assistant captains this year are AJ, Sammy, and Teddy," I said while the kids clapped after each name.

The excitement was still in the air as the players left for the ice. Forrest was the last player to leave the locker room and as he walked by I asked, "Are you ready Captain?"

"Watch this," Forrest said with a smile.

As the other players were skating around the rink to warm up, Forrest jumped on the ice, banged his stick three times, and yelled, "Here we go boys!" The team immediately took off full speed around the rink.

The new leader had arrived.

COACHING CHALLENGE #15: IDENTIFYING LEADERSHIP

1. How does your captain reflect the identity of your team?
2. What characteristics do you value in a captain?
3. How do you determine who the captain should be?
4. Do you know of any role models either in our area or in professional sports that you could have your captain research to expand his knowledge of leading people?
5. What can you do to create leadership situations for all the players on your team?

16

INCREASING PRACTICE PACE AND INTENSITY

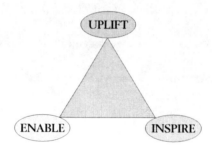

STRATEGY #16: UTILIZE AND MANIPULATE TIME AND SPACE IN PRACTICE

Continually challenge your players' ability by reducing and manipulating the time and space they have to work in.

IN OUR FIRST few games, offensively we were much more dangerous off the rush. When we got into the neutral zone with speed we created some good chances to score. However, our in-zone offensive game was poor. We didn't cycle the puck at all, we hadn't made a pass to the point in three games and we lost far too many one-on-one battles and races for loose pucks.

We weren't comfortable creating offense in confined space areas. When we were in the offensive zone, we would stand around and wait for good things to happen. The lack of puck support minimized our passing options. The puck carrier would just try to beat someone one-on-one and try to get to the net on his own.

There were going to be teams that would trap us, crowd the neutral zone and challenge us at the offensive blue-line. We needed to build confidence in a strong fore-check and low offensive game to give us offensive depth. Otherwise, we would turn the puck over at the offensive blue-line.

The first five or six practices of the year we ran flow-type practices. We used many assembly line drills, link drills and one puck-type drills. Early on, passing quality was the focus. We had got to the point where we were doing eight-minute drills without missing a pass. It was fun to watch, the kids were enjoying it, the practices flowed well and the pace was quick.

Before I was able to get into triangulation, cycling, screens, area passes, cross-dumps and the other offensive zone tactics, I needed to increase our team's ability to compete in small areas.

After talking it over with Bud and Tony, we decided that we needed to increase the intensity of practice. While the kids were developing into a tight team, they were also getting too comfortable and you could see them letting up on each other.

I knew four good ways to increase practice intensity that I learned from Coach Stone.

4 WAYS TO INCREASE PRACTICE INTENSITY

1. Design Live and Competitive drills
   - 'Live' meaning, no pre-determined pattern, like a game
   - Use 1 on 1, 2 on 2, 3 on 3 drills and games
   - Divide the group in half and keep score with friendly consequences (a lap to the losing team) to make it interesting and drive the spirit of competition.

2. Start with an undetermined possession
   - Start the drill with a race or battle for puck control
   - Players have to read and position themselves based on possession, but they won't know until it happens.

3. Reduce the amount of space available
   - Instead of giving them the whole ice or even a whole zone to work in, use corners and small areas.
   - Put more people in the drill or the area to help reduce the available space.

4. Reduce the amount of time available
   - Add back-pressure to the drill – create a chaser to reduce the time.

▨   ▨   ▨

Bud urged me for the two practices to mix more intensity into the practices, but I was apprehensive. I was feeling good about the chemistry of the team, they were showing signs of working together, and now we were going to pit them against each other. I was battling an inner struggle because I knew Bud was right, but I was worried we would unravel the cohesiveness we had built.

Tony suggested we do a modified game to end the next practice and see how the kids would respond. We could shorten the ice, divide the kids into two teams and play two-on-two. I thought that was a great compromise. The kids would undoubtedly have a ton of fun with it and it would be a great introduction into more competitive drills for the next couple of practices.

We set up the game to end the next practice and sure enough, the kids had a blast. It was amazing to see how the tenacious spirit came out in a few boys we didn't expect. The one that surprised us the most was Carter. We figured with the small ice he would really struggle, to our surprise he really competed hard.

Cain was also a surprise, we thought with the reduced ice, he'd take more contact and get pushed off the puck. He really stepped up his game, he used his skill to find open ice and he rolled off checks really well.

The player with the most skill in the tight area was Zack. He made some incredible passes and really showed a quick stick around the net.

Cliff and Bubba didn't fare so well; they got caught up in trying to be physical and they weren't able to be effective at all.

After that practice, we planned to add one new intensity drill format into each of the next four practices.

On the fifth practice, we set up the drills to progressively shrink the ice. We started with our assembly line and flow drill, moved to a chaser drill, and then we reduced the ice even further and started the drill with a race. The final drill was a confined space game.

It was neat to watch the intensity of the practice gradually build as we reduced the ice.

Bud suggested the next practice we do the reverse – progressively expand the ice.

We played around with the different formats to find a couple drills to which the kids would respond well. We made note of these drills so we could come back to them in future practices if practice needed a jolt of intensity.

This strategy sure beat screaming at them, or skating them to increase the intensity.

Drill structure and formations go a long way to determine the pace and intensity of the practice. I started strategically planning flow and planning intensity drills into certain parts of my practice design.

The payoff was immediate, there were times we competed harder in practice than we had in previous games. We really started to notice we were winning more loose pucks and battles in the next couple of games.

However, the best indication was when we were on the bench in one of the games. Brownie shouted down the bench to Robbie, "Hey Robbie, great hustle to win that race; you created that chance to score."

When the players started noticing and commenting on each other's ability to take what we learned in practice into a game we realized that it was sinking in.

COACHING CHALLENGE #16: TURNING UP THE HEAT

1. If teams play how they practice, what can you do to make practice a better reflection of your games?
2. What other ways do you know to improve the pace and intensity of practice?
3. Take one of your favorite flow drills and look for a way to create back-pressure.
4. Take a drill you would normally run full-ice and look for a way to squeeze the space available to them. Can you take the same drill and move it into the Neutral Zone using the width of the ice instead of the length of the ice?

17

TEACHING TO THE TOP

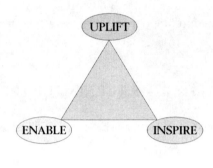

STRATEGY #17: CHALLENGE TALENT

Work hard to ensure the top end of your team is always being pushed to get better.

DURING PRACTICE, BUD and I are at opposite ends, which made his tap on my shoulder most surprising.

"Bud, what's the matter," I asked concerned.

"It's AJ, he hasn't lost a one-on-one battle in my end today," Bud said exasperated.

I turned and looked down in his end to see who AJ was competing with and saw Sammy.

"What about Sammy?" I asked thinking my top defenseman would pose a challenge.

"We have to do something to challenge him," Bud said shaking his head.

With our focus on competitiveness, intensity, winning battles and winning races, the other players had much more to gain by AJ competition. We needed to bring someone in who could challenge and motivate him.

It was time to call John to invite players from the Bantam team to skate with us during practice. A few players on that team have the size to pose a challenge and it was time to invite them out.

When I talked to John in August about AJ and his development, he said there would come a time when we would have to do more for him. That time was now.

After speaking with John, I gave John our schedule for the month and extended an open invitation for players to come out.

Even if the Bantam team could send as many as five or six players (three forwards, two defensemen and a goalie) out, our practices would gain tremendously with the extra skill on the ice. It would give all of our players a chance to work with them. It could turn out to be a mentorship of sorts. I was certain the older players would be grateful for the extra ice.

The Bantam coach was eager to get his players some extra ice. When I suggested that he could send a whole line, a couple of defense and a goalie he was surprised. He offered for us to do the same with his team, where we could send five or six players out to his practice in return.

It's easier to run a four line, eight defenseman practice, than it is to run a three line, six defenseman practice.

Both of us were excited to work together. While I don't think it is a rare occurrence for coaches of different levels to work together, we don't do it as much as we should.

We had talked to our team beforehand to explain the purpose of having these players out. We wanted to do our best to make them feel welcome.

Our players were excited; it is natural for them to want to test themselves against the next level.

We started with some assembly line drills. What was interesting was the reaction of our players when one of the older guys missed a pass, he would just pick up another puck. Bud was heading over to let them know that we did things differently around here, when our players in the line filled him in on how we only play one puck in practice.

We then broke into our groups for small space competitive drills and everyone was anxious to see how AJ would stack up against the Bantams.

We ran a basic one-on-one, puck protection style, drill out of a circle. Bud skated over to AJ's Bantam opponent before it was their turn and said to him, "Hey, make sure you teach this kid a lesson, he's running all over our league and we need to show him what the next level looks like. Don't take it easy on him; make him earn every inch."

The boy nodded as the whistle went for his turn to start.

To say that AJ performed admirably is an understatement. The change in his focus and his determination was amazing. This was an AJ that we weren't accustomed to seeing. It was clear that he needed this challenge on a regular basis. He had earned the respect of the Bantams.

For the first time we had seen AJ at his best. There were times where he dominated the Bantams; it became obvious that he was just scratching the surface of what he could become.

Our job as coaches became clear; we needed to challenge him all the time. By inviting the Bantams out, that was a step in the right direction, but we couldn't limit ourselves to that, we needed to find out more about AJ's capabilities.

Accelerating a player to the next age group is a delicate process; you have to be very careful that you aren't pushing too fast. For AJ, he loved his teammates and there was still another level of performance for him to accomplish. If we could continue to supplement his development by surrounding him with more talent, we would go a long way to help him realize his potential.

I spoke to the Bantam Coach and he was impressed with AJ and Sammy as well. Both had handled themselves well during the practice and the Bantam Coach suggested that we start looking at getting both AJ and Sammy some games at his level. I couldn't agree more.

The relationship with the Bantam team continued to grow throughout the season. All of our players had numerous opportunities to practice with them and there were very few practices we didn't have at least one Bantam out.

To take it a step further we built a relationship with the Peewee A team. We wanted to create a development relationship with them that mirrored what we were doing with the Bantams.

Every team has a top end and a bottom end, but aligning ourselves with the team above us, we were able to continue to challenge and provide development opportunity for the top of our team.

At the same time, when we aligned ourselves with the team below us, we were able to provide mentorship and leadership opportunity for all the players on our team.

We had added at least one and sometimes two extra ice times for the players on our team to develop. Our kids were excited to have the chance to challenge, or be the challenge every week.

COACHING CHALLENGE #17: CHALLENGING THE TOP OF YOUR TEAM

1. What ideas do you have that would increase the development challenges for your top players?

2. How can you improve your relationship with the coach of the team above you so he will feel comfortable to lend you players from his team to your practices and/or invite your players to attend his practices?
3. How can you use the Affiliated Player System to present new challenges to your top players?
4. What can you do to encourage older players to want to come to your practices?

18

LEAVE NO ONE BEHIND

STRATEGY #18: LEAVE NO ONE BEHIND

Take a teaching approach to challenges. A teacher is always looking for ways to reach their students more effectively.

JOHN CALLED ME unexpectedly one night at home. He asked me, "What's the biggest problem or challenge you have with your team right now?"

I thought for a moment and responded, "The biggest challenge is getting a couple of our players to play to their strengths."

"Give me an example," John said probingly.

"Well take Teddy, here's a player who has no idea what type of player he could be," I said.

"What are you going to do about it?" John asked challenging me.

After fumbling around with some answers, the truth was I hadn't put any thought into what to do about it. I recognized the problem, but didn't spend any time figuring out how to address it.

John proceeded to quiz me, "Have you heard his perspective? What type of player does he believe he is right now? Where do you project him? Have you communicated that to him?"

The conversation with John highlighted that I had to take more responsibility and be more proactive in trying to help my players. The easy part was diagnosing the problem; the hard part was working with the player to create a solution.

Teddy represented a development project on our team that had the most potential to make a big difference in a short period of time. Here was a player who had excellent size and strength. He was a very good skater who had a rocket of a shot. He had all the makings of becoming an elite power forward.

Teddy was a player whose physical skills and ability could make an impact in a game in many ways. His speed and aggressive nature made him an excellent fore-checker. He was fearless and he was one of the few players who would drive the net without the puck. He could be in front of the net on the power play and had good enough hand eye coordination to tip, deflect and play rebounds. Teddy had the ability to be an intimidating presence on the ice and needed to find ways to use the ice that he had earned through his aggressive play more effectively.

The problem was he had no idea; he believed he was an enforcer. He thought his job was to run shotgun with the top player on his team and make sure nobody took physical liberties against him. Therefore, he was always in the penalty box because he was so easy to goad into a penalty.

When we looked at our first eight games of the season, Teddy was by far the leading penalty minute man on our team. While we didn't like to see him in the penalty box, that's not what bothered us the most. It was the kinds of penalties he was taking, nearly every penalty was a reaction type penalty; roughing after the whistle developed into his favorite, closely followed by retaliatory slashing, roughing, and high sticking not to mention the string of unsportsmanlike conduct penalties and ten-minute misconducts.

I was the first to say that I didn't mind players playing aggressively but this to me was not aggressive; this was being stupid.

I talked it over with Bud who had a handle on the situation. Bud in his playing days broke into Junior as a fighter in the Quebec Major Junior Hockey League. He was the only English-speaking player on his team. In those days, it was like attending the school of hard knocks and paying for the education with your blood! He had quickly learned the role of the enforcer and had spent time after his playing days studying the role as it continued to evolve. He had worked his way from a rookie fourth line goon into a fourth year energy player. He had developed some strong feelings and had a theory of how players get categorized for the various roles.

Here is a profile we developed of the physical roles on a hockey team.

At the bottom of the list is the enforcer role. This role is being somewhat phased out of hockey. While fighting may never leave the game entirely, with each passing year it is becoming less and less of a priority for teams to carry players whose primary ability is to fight. The demand is becoming greater for players to be able to bring other hockey value and fulfill other more diverse roles on a hockey team is becoming greater.

Then there is the energy player role. The energy player is a physical fore-checker who loves to initiate contact. He is valuable to the team because combined with the right line-mates, this type of player can pick up the intensity and change the momentum of the game with a single high-energy shift or a well-timed hit. They are usually great penalty killers and assume a more defensive role on a hockey team thus making the value of their role more diverse.

Then there is the power forward. The power forward is a player who is very physical player on the puck. Generally a physical fore-checker, a skilled player in the ten to fifteen feet from the offensive net, and will drive the net with and without the puck. The power forward type player is a presence on every shift. They tend to create a ton of space with their physical play and willingness to drive the net.

The difference between an energy player and a power forward is that an energy player is physical when he is in pursuit of the puck. A power forward is physical when he has the puck.

Bud and I were convinced that Teddy was playing like an enforcer, when he had the skills of a power forward. Our challenge was to convince him that he could grow into the power forward role with just a few adjustments to his game. Most of the adjustments were mental, as the physical skills seemed to be there.

We taped some NHL games to show Teddy the difference in roles. To start the tape we had clips of all three types of players. Then we had game film of him. What we wanted to do was give him a current NHL power forward role model to pattern his game. The video not only illustrated our point, but also motivated him to develop the skills needed to fulfill the role.

I wanted Bud to take the lead because he had developed a good relationship with Teddy. Bud would tell him stories of his days in the Quebec League and Teddy had a great deal of respect for Bud. I felt the time was right for Bud to use his relationship with Teddy as a development tool.

We brought him in and showed him the video and Bud asked him, "So which one of these three NHL guys do you think your game most resembles?"

Teddy believed that his role was to 'serve and protect.'

We then took him back to our parent/player meeting and brought out our initial evaluation sheet of him. It talked about the potential we saw in him to be an offensive player. We wrote that we thought he "had power forward written all over him."

Bud then brought out the game sheets of our first eight games which he had highlighted Teddy's penalties and asked Teddy what he thought of his penalties.

Teddy acknowledged that he had taken too many penalties but he thought, "It was important early on in the season to establish a physical presence for AJ."

We talked about how we would like to see him alter his game to be more effective. Here is a summary of the points we wanted to build into Teddy's game.

1. Initiate physical play inside the context of the game instead of reacting to someone else and retaliating. Start by finishing every check and drive the net without the puck.

2. Invest in fore-check contacts on defensemen. By creating contact with their defensemen early on in the game, they may begin to hear your footsteps and make poor decisions with the puck.

3. Draw penalties because you are driving the net with and without the puck. In practice, work on developing a power move with the puck on both the fore-hand and the back-hand.

4. Work hard to stay on the ice; you have no presence when you are in the penalty box. If you take a penalty make sure it's because you were trying to do something positive; goaltender interference because you drove the net too hard, charging or boarding because you took too many steps on the fore-check, or interference because you were using your size to set a pick.

5. Make a point of arriving at the front of their net every time you cross the offensive blue-line. Spend time in practice working on rebounds, tips and deflections; in the assembly line drills, stop in front of the net and play the next shot coming to the net.

6. Start thinking and playing like a power forward. Instead of concerning yourself with protecting AJ, work to create space for him; set picks and screens, drive the net.

7. Work the front of the net on the power play

These are the characteristics of a physical player. If Teddy drove the net consistently and finished every check, he would become infinitely more valuable.

We expected it to be a slow process but in three games, we would meet again and match up the NHL power forward tape with his game tape. Every game we would try to add a new dimension to his game, to build his skill profile to match that of an elite power forward.

Teddy's problem was the limited view of his role and of what playing tough really was. Toughness is the space you create for yourself and your teammates by presence. Teddy needed to realize that he had no presence when he was sitting in the penalty box.

Once I took responsibility that it was my job to find a way to communicate my thoughts to Teddy, everything fell into place.

COACHING CHALLENGE #18: LEAVE NO ONE BEHIND

1. Identify a player on your team that you feel needs to learn to use his strengths more effectively. What can you do to help that player make little adjustments to his game to be more effective?
2. List all the things you can do and the resources you have available to you to help the player understand and make these adjustments.
3. Identify a player who has a limited view of his value to the team. What can you do to help the player realize that he is limiting his potential and inspire him to aspire to become much more?
4. List all the ways you can communicate an expanded role for this player.

19

IMPROVE STICK SKILLS

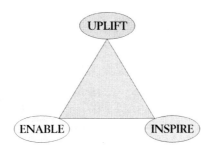

STRATEGY #19: IMPROVE STICK SKILLS

Knowing what hand players shoot and knowing what hand is their dominant hand in life, is the first step to building elite stick skill.

IN THE SECOND month of the season, John held the second in a series of coaching seminars. These seminars were a good excuse for all the coaches in the association to get together and discuss hockey development issues.

In August, he hosted the first of these seminars, 'The 3 Speeds of Hockey', which we applied in our player selection process. I found getting together periodically during the season to discuss development ideas and concepts very helpful.

Invariably during the season, there are issues that come up with your hockey team that you aren't sure how to deal with. When you are in a room with twenty coaches who have over a hundred years of coaching experience between them, someone will have an idea that challenges the way you think of various aspects of the game. I found value and inspiration in each of the seminars.

This month's seminar centered on developing stick skills. John presented theory, technical information and approaches to developing stick handling, quick release shooting, passing and pass receiving skills. While I picked up a little something on each of the topics, the most revealing was his discussion on the link between the hand a player shoots and his dominant hand in every day life. It was a fascinating discussion that changed the way I approach stick skill development.

Based solely on the relationship between the hand they shoot and their dominant hand in life, some players have a distinct advantage over other players in their rate of stick skill development.

For example, players whose dominant hand is their right hand: that is, they write and throw a ball with their right hand, but are left handed shots in hockey have a distinct advantage over those players whose dominant hand is the same as the hand they shoot with.

The advantage lies in the dominant hand being the top hand on the stick. For developing elite puck skills, it is ideal for the top hand on the stick to be the dominant hand because it is the hand that controls the skill aspect of the movement of the stick blade. The bottom hand of the stick must move freely up and down the shaft of the stick, increasing and decreasing stick skill range as well as applying varying degrees of pressure on the shaft.

Players whose dominant hand is the bottom hand when holding the stick have an immediate challenge to overcome. They must resist the natural tendency to control the stick blade with the bottom hand and train the top hand to execute the skill movements of the blade. This is difficult to change.

A common term in every hockey circle is 'cement hands'. 'Cement hands' to me refers to the intensity of the grip of the bottom hand. These players are quick to find on the ice; they are the ones who are 'chopping snakes' or slapping the ice with their stick while handling the puck. If you see players having difficulty rolling their wrists when handling the puck or the bottom hand on their sticks stays in the same spot on the shaft when they are handling the puck, this means they are controlling the stick blade with their bottom hands.

This is significant because the definition of elite stick skills is high speed and wide range movements with the premium on range at high skating speed, or the width a player uses when handling the puck tactically. Most players handle the puck comfortably inside their skates or shoulder width; elite stick skill is a player's skill level with the puck when it is outside of his skates. Players who control the stick blade with their bottom hand will have difficulty with any puck skill movements outside of their skates because of how reluctant they are to allow the bottom hand to move freely up and down the shaft.

John gave an example of the most talented player with whom he had ever worked and who wrote left-handed, threw a ball right handed and was a right-handed shot. He believed that the ambidextrous nature or balance of strength in his hands made him pre-disposed to acquire stick skills quickly and more naturally than others.

One of the rarities in hockey is a highly skilled right-handed shot either on defense or a forward, most centers are left handed, which is likely in direct proportion to the number of right-handed people in general.

His point was players whose dominant hand is their top hand have a more natural opportunity to acquire stick skills when all else is comparatively equal.

The challenge from a coaching perspective is to identify these characteristics in our players and be sensitive to the development needs of those whose dominant hand is the low hand on their stick. For these players to develop elite stick skills they will need their top hand to control the stick blade. This is a difficult process, but if we catch it soon enough we can prevent the early limitations that this has on a player's stick skill potential.

When you watch young players with a puck, they handle it side-to-side using only a 2 or 3 foot area when they stick-handle. To develop stickhandling skills, we must encourage players to be creative and to handle the puck outside their skates, especially to the backhand side. If a player does handle the puck outside his skates, it is usually on the forehand. There are nine stick handling locations available to a player. The two most common areas are middle front and forehand side, but it is a player's ability to handle the puck effectively in each of the other four areas and the speed he has in moving from one area to another that truly defines a player's ability to handle the puck.

The other limitation that players have relative to their stick skill development is that young players generally stickhandle in time with the pace and the rhythm of their skates.

What that means is that players tend to stickhandle in time with their skating. The limitation that this habit develops is that when the player attempts to do anything tactical he must stop his feet to execute the stick skill. Examples of this include:

1. When you watch a young player shoot the puck, what does he do in the moment prior to shooting? He stops his feet and glides to move the puck from the front of his body to the forehand side.
2. What does a young player do in the moment prior to passing or receiving a pass? He stops his feet and glides to release or receive the puck.
3. In the moment prior to deking or executing a one-on-one move, what

is common to see in young players? They stop their feet to execute the stick skill and when the move is finished, they resume skating.

The ability to separate the players' hands from their feet is a critical stage in the development of elite stick skills. We must stress to all of our athletes to learn to keep their feet moving when executing all stick skills; whether it is passing, receiving a pass, shooting or deking.

The opportunity to learn these kinds of elite stick skills during the formative years of development is the gift that we must provide all of our athletes.

The next practice after the seminar, I had Tony on a mission to find out the dominant hand of each of our players and the hand that they shoot. Bud, Tony and I found the results very interesting.

Figure 4:

STICK SKILL CHART			
Player	Shoots	Dominant Hand	Stick Skill Notes
AJ	Right	Left	Highly skilled player with the puck, can execute all stick skills with his feet moving.
Teddy	Right	Right	Excellent shooter, poor one-on-one stick skill creativity
Cain	Left	Right	Very good puck skills, very smooth and can execute all stick skills except for shooting while his feet are moving.
Forrest	Left	Right	Average puck skills, has difficulty releasing the puck with his feet moving
Zack	Left	Right	Excellent puck skills, has difficulty keeping his feet moving when releasing the puck
Adam	Left	Right	Best stickhandling range of any player on the team, has difficulty keeping his feet moving when releasing the puck.

Robbie	Right	Right	Lacks confidence in puck skills.
Brock	Left	Right	Very good one-on-one skills, weak shot
Matt	Left	Right	Poor creativity with the puck, weak shot
Sammy	Left	Right	Outstanding puck skills, great shot, smooth passer with his feet moving
Carter	Right	Right	Quick stick, really lacks range.
Brownie	Left	Right	Good puck skills, weak shot
Bubba	Left	Left	Excellent power in his shot, no stickhandling range
Cliff	Right	Right	Excellent power in his shot, no stickhandling range
Reese	Left	Right	Average puck skills, weak shot

What we noticed from our chart was that AJ had that rare combination that made him the most predisposed to elite stick skills and he had developed at an accelerated rate.

What was surprising was the number of players we identified on our team who have poor stick handling range and the number of players we identified who had weak shots.

The player with the hardest shot on our team was Teddy and his dominant hand was the low hand on the stick.

Three of our six defensemen were bottom hand dominant.

Clearly, we had a lot of work to do with our team to provide them with the opportunity to acquire elite stick skills.

Our practice focus would be as follows:

- Teach and encourage the players to use in-stride shots in practice
- Make sure we start every practice with a five-minute creative stick-handling drill that encourages them to handle the puck outside of their shoulder width.
  - o Spend the extra time with Teddy, Robbie, Bubba, Carter and Cliff to

help them get their bottom hand moving more freely up and down the shaft

- Add in-stride passing and pass receiving to our flow and assembly line drills.

We knew what we had to do and we were committed to making the adjustments in practice to help the players improve their stick skills.

COACHING CHALLENGE #19: IMPROVING STICK SKILLS

1. Make a chart similar to the one in this chapter to determine the dominant hand and the top hand of each of your players. How many players' bottom hand is their dominant hand?
2. What on-ice drills can you do to help these players soften their bottom hand so it moves effectively up and down the shaft of the stick?
3. What off-ice drills can you give your players to help soften their bottom hand and strengthen their top hand?

20

THE THREE SKILL SPEEDS OF HOCKEY

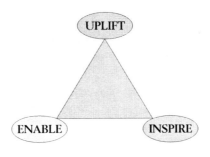

STRATEGY #20: DEVELOP THE THREE SKILL SPEEDS OF HOCKEY

*Invest in the three skill speeds, focusing on developing the skill speed in combination;
they are fundamental to expanding their ability to perform at the next level.*

IN THEORY, SEPARATING players' hands from their feet sounded good. I understood the theory and identified with the examples. The more I thought about it the more excited I was to begin the process with our players. That's where the difficulty came.

How do you retrain a player who has ingrained a habit into his game for the last eight or ten years? The practical challenges to affect this change were unbelievable. I wasn't sure where to start.

I decided to give John a call to see if he had more information on how I could begin to implement this with our team.

John started by saying, "Make sure every player either has a puck on their stick or is expecting to get one the entire practice, that's a start." He went on to describe the following process.

"To help players separate their hands from their feet you need to make sure you are always combining two skill speeds at any one time during practice."

I remembered our first seminar on the three speeds of hockey, where John suggested that players play at the level of their weakest skill speed. I was able to use that information to help project the development of players in the selection process. The next step was to learn how to incorporate the three skill speeds into our development plan.

John continued. "The same way players play at the level of their weakest skill speed, they execute skill combinations at the level of their weakest skill speed. A player, who skates significantly faster than he can handle the puck, will need to slow down his skating speed in order to execute puck skills. It is critical that you are always challenging your players with skill combinations."

"The trick to separating the players' hands from their feet lies in your ability as a coach to create full-speed skill situations. In other words, by encouraging your players to perform puck skills and decisions while skating at their top speed, you are forcing them out of their comfort zone. The more a player performs puck skills on the outer edges of their skating speed, the faster the elite skill development."

I interjected. "Let me get this straight. What you are telling me is to separate the players' hands from their feet I need them to skate faster? I would have thought the opposite. I would have thought I would need to slow them down and teach through a progression."

John responded, "This is where most coaches make a mistake in developing elite skill. Their first instinct is to slow the player down, which is exactly the opposite of what needs to be done to build skill at this level."

"If you want players to learn to skate faster you must get them on the outer edges of where they feel comfortable, everything else is build-up. The real development in skating speed only occurs once the player is uncomfortable. When players start to settle into a speed they previously felt uneasy, that's development. If you allow players to continue to skate at levels where they feel secure they have little opportunity to improve.

"To develop elite puck skills, the only opportunity for that development to occur is when we have the player in full flight with the puck. Until we get the player to that level, we aren't making progress."

"The challenge for you as a coach is to create an environment where falling down and being on the edge of out of control is cool. If a player feels that it is acceptable to fail when learning, he will continually push the outer limits of his ability. That's what we don't do enough of as coaches."

I started to understand, but still needed more clarification. "So let me ask you this, once we get the player to go the outer edges of his speed with the puck what do we do next?"

John laughed. "Well, that's when we ask them to perform the elements and characteristics of elite puck skill."

- Releasing –passing or shooting—and receiving a puck at full speed
- Changing direction both laterally and in transition without slowing down prior.
- Attacking one-on-one without breaking stride.
- Locating and skating to open ice in crowded situations without breaking stride.

"These are all characteristics of elite skill; you have to find ways to build those development opportunities into practice for your players."

"You know I'm going to ask you your suggestions on how I can do that," I said

"I had a feeling that was coming," John said excitedly. "And lucky for you I have a few ideas. I have two tips that you should incorporate into every practice from now to the end of the season."

1. Make sure all in every drill, every player either has a puck on his stick or is expecting to get one.
2. Take time every practice, whether it is at the beginning, the end or strategically timed within the structure of your practice to do 8's

"Ok, hold on a minute, John," I interrupted. "What are 8's?"

John quickly responded. "8's are figure 8 skating patterns that you do every practice. The goal of 8's is to use the circular pattern to encourage cross-over striding to help get your players to full speed with the puck."

"Coaches have used the five circle skating drill since the beginning of time. The problem I have with the five circles is the quality of the last two circles isn't usually the same as the first two. By doing 8's you focus on two circles and work towards quality and speed."

"The teaching point with 8's is to make sure that your players continue skating in the corners of the 8. An easy way to test your players' willingness to challenge themselves at full speed is to see how they skate the 8's. Many players will skate the straightaway and glide in the arc because the arc is uncomfortable. This, of course, is the exact opposite of what you want."

"The best part about 8's is you can do them forwards, backwards, with transitions, the only limit is your imagination. You could go all season doing 8's and never do the same one twice."

Figure 5:

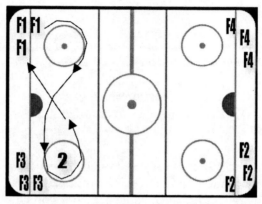

'END ZONE 8'S' DRILL

Divide team into four corners.

Send everyone in the corner at the same time to create a more competitive and clustered environment.

Encourage players to skate the corners at full speed.

The key is for the players to continue skating and crossing over through corner 2.

The faster you go the lower and wider you need to be.

■   ▩   ▩

John drew an end zone 8's drill and said, "Now take this basic 8's drill and move it around – take it into the neutral zone, confine the space, etc."

"I got it now," I said urging John to continue.

"Add back-pressure to all one-on-one drills," explained John.

"You mean a back-checker right?" I asked for confirmation.

"Yes," John said, "you want to pressure the player to move forward and attack with speed. One of the problems with the way we traditionally do one-on-ones is there is no back-pressure so the attacker feels free to attack at a comfortable pace. In a game of course, the one-on-one advantage is under pressure, so we want our players to practice that way as well."

Figure 6:

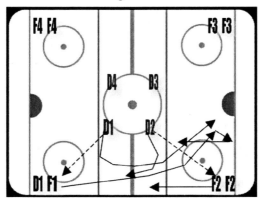

BACKPRESSURE 1 ON 1 DRILL

D1 passes to F1 who attacks D1 1 on 1 to the net, after the play finishes at the net, D2 passes to F2 and defends him 1 on 1. F1 stops at the net after his shot and backchecks to put back pressure on F2 as he attacks the goal. This is continuous from both sides.

▩   ▩   ▩

Then John explained another drill. "By taking a standard 1 on 1 drill and having the attacking forward backcheck, the next play puts pressure on the attacker to build speed and attack aggressively."

"I understand," I said suggesting I was ready to move on.

"Make in-stride shots and in-stride passes the rule of practice. Let them shoot their fair share of slap shots, but make those drills fun and separate from what you are trying to achieve in most of your practices which is quick release shots and passes."

"Those adjustments should be easy to integrate into our regular practice format," I said thinking ahead.

John continued to share the association changes on Multi-tasking. "We are making changes in our practice structure at the early ages to help with this development at an early age."

"For example, by the end of this month we will have a puck on the stick of every player in every practice for all of our introductory programs in the system."

"For years, we have been following the ancient system of teaching a player to skate first and then give him the puck afterwards. That development approach, while well-intentioned, is not effective."

"What do you mean it's not effective, it sounds like a logical approach for kids who are just starting?" I added.

"Not really," John said. "Let me ask you this, and I'm certain you will answer your own question."

"Take a player who has been power-skating in the off- season. What happens to that player's skating when you introduce a puck to him?"

"Well, he slows down," I answered.

"Exactly! Do you know why?" John asked quickly.

"No, I really don't," I answered honestly.

John continued to make his point. "It's because when players have the puck, they have two hands on their stick and the stick on the ice, which makes them carry their body differently than when they don't have a puck."

"Let me ask you this … When you see someone teaching power skating, what is the instruction relative to the arms?"

"Swing them," I answered confidently.

"Do they swing their arms in time or coordinate with their skating in any way?" John asked.

"Yeah, usually opposite arm to opposite skate," I answered starting to see where all this was going.

"So you are saying that when we teach power skating without the puck and teach them to swing their arms in time with their stick handling we are in effect training the player to link their hands with their feet?" I asked.

"You got it!" John praised. "That is why it is so important to do all of our skating, skating instruction, and even skating correction, with a puck. It provides opportunity for the player to separate his hands from his feet much earlier in their development."

"Wow, I understand completely," I said wanting John to know that I had captured his point.

"So how do we encourage the power skating instructors that work with our teams to use pucks and teach the players to separate their hands from their feet?" I asked as the question popped into my head.

"Well, I suppose if they want to continue to work with our teams, they will teach skating skills in combination with the puck, now won't they?" John said with a smile.

After my conversation with John, I had a new focus. I knew the basics to incorporate multi-tasking into our practices.

I was excited to try it out in our next practice.

COACHING CHALLENGE #20: SEPARATING THE PLAYERS' HANDS FROM THEIR FEET

1. List all the skills that require the players to separate their hands from their feet.
2. Design a drill for each of the skills you listed.
3. Take each drill and find a way to create pressure on the puck carrier to increase speed.

21

Role Diversification

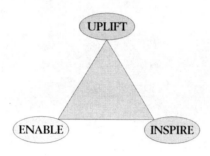

STRATEGY #21: DEVELOP THE COMPLETE PLAYER

Make it a priority to ensure that all players can play in all situations. Versatility is a wonderful gift any coach can give his players.

WE WERE UP one goal, late in the game against the first place team. I had been rolling my lines the entire game as usual except for two penalty-killing situations and the last minute of the game. In each case, I passed over Cain in favor of Matt.

We won the game against a team that our team hadn't beaten on the road in two years. The team from the staff, the players and the parents were excited about the win. Everyone was excited, except Cain.

Cain was trying hard to hide his personal disappointment and share in the team celebration, but Bud pointed him out to me when we were in the dressing room and I knew why he was upset. I decided to go over talk to him.

"Hey Cain, that was a big win eh?" I said to break the ice.

"Yeah," he said quietly and without looking up.

"Is there something you want to talk to me about?" I asked hoping to engage him in conversation, as I was anxious to tell him why I had passed him over.

"No, I'm alright Coach," he said doing his best to get me to leave.

"Cain, you can talk to me, why don't you meet me in the stands in five minutes?" I said pushing the issue.

"Ok," he replied uncertainly.

I then sent Tony to find Cain's parents to let them know that I was going to have a chat with him before they left.

"So you want to ask me why I passed you over for those two third period penalty kills and the last minute," I asked.

Cain looked up and said, "Yeah."

I took a second and then began to walk him through my reasoning.

"Well, if the situation was reversed and we were the team needing a goal you'd be one of the first guys I would want on the ice because you are skilled. You create chances to score, and you are dangerous from anywhere on the ice."

"When we are killing an important penalty or we are protecting a tight lead late in the game, I don't have the same desire to put you on the ice. That is mostly because I don't have much confidence in your defensive awareness, commitment and skills in those situations."

"For example, in the first period tonight I needed you to take a hit to make an important chip out and your lack of effort let their defenseman keep the puck in. In the second period, you were the weak-side forward in our zone. You decided to cheat and leave the zone early, resulting in a quality chance from the high slot. In the third period, after spending half a shift in our own zone, I needed you to dump the puck and change and you chose to carry it one against two."

"We talked about this on the bench the last couple of games and you aren't making the adjustment. As long as you continue to play one-way you will get passed over when there are defensive situations, like tonight."

"Now, you have two choices. You can make an effort to learn to be more responsible defensively and earn the confidence of your teammates in defensive situations or you can continue to do what you are doing and when those situations come up, you can watch someone else do it."

His eyes met mine for the first time, as he knew I was challenging him. Now that I had his attention, I decided to make my point about role diversification, which is the next step in his development.

"Cain, you are an excellent offensive hockey player, but defensively you don't apply yourself with the same enthusiasm. That needs to change if you want to pursue the elite levels of hockey."

"Let me ask you this. How many roles on a hockey team could you fulfill?"

"What do you mean?" he asked.

"I mean, you are a left shooting left-winger right?"

"Yeah," he confirmed

"Can you play center or right wing?" I asked, building my case.

"I don't know I've never tried," he said.

"With the way you play now, there is no way you could play in a checking role on a team, right?" I said looking for confirmation.

"Right," he said looking confused.

"Here is my point Cain. Right now on any team you try out for, you are there only for two roles in the line-up that you fill."

"Which ones are those?" he asked.

"First or second line scoring left-winger, all other spots in the line-up are energy roles or positions you don't play," I responded.

"My question to you is, what happens if there are two veteran, offensively-proven left wingers on the team already, where does that put you?" I asked.

"I don't know," he said honestly.

"Neither do I," I said with a smile. "Here's what I do know. I know that you are a competitive person and you don't want to be passed over for any ice at any time in a game. I also know that you are a smart and talented hockey player, who if you put your mind to something, will learn very quickly. I also think that you could be a very good hockey player and it saddens me to see you limit yourself in this way," I continued, starting to build him up.

"I want to help you become more of a complete player so when someone else asks you how many spots you could play in a line-up; your answer would be 'I can play any forward position and any role on a hockey team. I want to play where I can help the team the most' and have the game to back it up," I said, as he nodded in agreement.

"There may come a time in your career when you are not going to be in an offensive role. Someone is going to pick you for your offensive potential, but not play you in that role initially. To get on the ice, you are going to have to excel in the defensive parts of the game, until you get the opportunity to play in an offensive role," I said continuing to illustrate my point.

"I do not want you to get in that situation and be unprepared to compete. You need to develop this part of your game so you can excel in whatever role you start in. The next step in your development as a player is to learn how to be defensively aware and responsible, and be able to turn good defensive plays into offensive opportunities. I would like to help you, but you have to meet me halfway. You have to want to be in any important situation in a game. What do you say?" I asked hoping I had made my point clearly.

"I say I never want to get passed over again, and I will work hard to improve that part of my game so you will have confidence in me," Cain said emphatically.

"That's what I thought you'd say," I said with a smile.

This was the first time in Cain's hockey career that he had had to be defensively aware and responsible. I was anxious to see his response in practice. We were going to test him right away. I knew he would rise to the challenge; most kids do. Really, they only give you what you ask of them.

COACHING CHALLENGE #21:

1. On your team, how many roles can each of your players fulfill?
2. How many players on your team do you trust in the last minute of a game when you are both up a goal and down a goal?
3. List two ways you can approach a player who you feel needs to be more committed defensively.

22

WHEN A FORWARD IS A DEFENSEMAN AND VICE VERSA

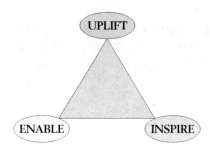

STRATEGY #22: CHALLENGE PLAYERS TO PLAY DIFFERENT POSITIONS

Expand the potential of a player on your team by experimenting to reveal the position/ role that best suits his strengths.

WE WERE EXCITED for the Christmas tournament. We had an opportunity to play some of the best teams in Ontario, Detroit, Connecticut, New York and Philadelphia. There were some outstanding teams and incredible individual talent. We were happy to have had the opportunity to be there and we were determined to leave an impression.

Through the first three games, we were 3 and 0 and playing the best hockey that we had played to that point in the season. It was rewarding to watch our players compete with the best that the tournament had to offer.

In the fourth game, we ran into a physical and skilled hockey team. They were also 3 and 0 and the winner of this game would advance to the tournament play-offs. It wasn't long into the game when Bud leaned into me and said, "We better start thinking about what we are going to do about Reese."

"Don't you think he can overcome the physical mismatch?" I asked.

"They are matching their three biggest and most physical forwards against him and they have dumped it in his corner every time to invest in some contacts. He's going to wear down quick if this keeps up," Bud said with concern.

"Let me change the match-up and see if that helps," I said trying to find a way to combat the excellent coaching strategy.

I changed the match-ups and their coach changed right with me. He was determined to exploit Reese.

"I don't think we can keep putting him out there; his risk for injury is getting higher with each shift. They had four good hits on him last shift alone," Bud said obviously concerned.

"What about getting Brownie to set some screens to give Reese more time to get behind the net," I said hoping to explore all solutions.

"Brownie has set a good screen on every dump in so far, the problem is they send two guys every time," Bud explained.

"What about bringing Matt back on defense and putting Reese up front? That line needs a change anyways," I said running out of suggestions.

"I like that," Bud said in support. "Matt is our best defensive forward; it's worth a try."

I then asked Matt if he'd ever played any defense. He said he filled in a couple times last year and said he liked it. That was all I needed to hear to make the switch. What we didn't account for was how Reese would respond to playing forward.

Reese started his first shift out with Robbie and Brock by winning a face-off cleanly. It was the first time that line started with the puck all year. We'd tried Robbie, Brock and Matt in the face-off circle and they couldn't win a draw if all three of them were taking the face-off together. Reese went in and won the first one cleanly, which got our attention.

I don't think anyone realized how fast Reese really was; his speed was much more noticeable when he was moving forward. He used his speed effectively on both the fore-check and the back-check. He caught a guy from behind in the neutral zone in each of his first two shifts. Most impressive was how quickly he was able to jump in the rush on the breakout.

He was always a good passer, but as a forward he seemed more comfortable to hang onto the puck a little longer to make a play. There were a couple times he won a loose puck with his speed, skated to open ice, and made a play to the net.

It was clear that while he had some positional issues as a forward, his strengths as a player were highlighted more as a forward than they were as a defenseman.

He was tenacious on the puck and used his speed effectively. He created offensive chances to score, was very responsible defensively, won face-offs and more importantly was able to bring out the best in himself and his line mates. It was by far the best game that Brock had played; he fed off the speed of Robbie and Reese and found a way to complement them, and he seemed better able to read Reese than Matt.

It seemed like a natural move for him. I was anxious after the game to hear his thoughts.

"Hey Reese, you looked comfortable as a forward," I started.

"Yeah, I felt good out there, I really liked playing with Robbie and Brock, and I thought we were going to get one," he said with excitement as he referred to some missed chances at the net for a goal.

"I thought your speed and aggressiveness was much more noticeable as a forward than it ever was as a defenseman. What did you think?" I asked probingly.

"I like playing forward, when I was younger my Dad wanted me to play defense because he felt there was more opportunity for me to play. Now that I haven't grown very much we both knew I was going to have to make the switch sooner or later," Reese said knowingly.

"Well do you want to try it for a few more games and see what happens?" I asked.

"Sure, that would be fun," he said with a grin.

There was no question that Reese's days as a defenseman were numbered. It was only a matter of time before his size would catch up to him; he just didn't have the offensive ability to survive as an undersized defenseman. However, as a forward his prospects grew immensely. He became the prototypical energy player who could kill penalties, pressure the puck and win face-offs.

As impressive as Reese was at center, even more impressive was Matt back on defense.

Matt is an excellent athlete, he has good size, great work ethic, and an unselfish team-first attitude; he is intelligent and therefore very coach-able.

The weaknesses in his game as a forward were that he couldn't score and he didn't see the ice very well. He tended to play a simple and defensive-oriented game, which made him a reliable player for the coach.

When we put him back on defense, a new set of skills emerged from Matt that we did not see when he was a forward.

The biggest difference in him was his ice vision. As a center-man, he continually made poor passing decisions the deeper he was in the offensive end. It seemed like the smaller the space the poorer the pass. As a defenseman, he looked like a quarterback; he made good decisions with the puck and seemed much more comfortable reading the play from back there.

What was interesting is that as a defenseman, his biggest strength was his ice vision, but as a forward it was his biggest weakness. I think the paradox has to do with vantage point. As a defenseman with the puck, the entire play is in front of him, but as a forward deep in the offensive zone, he is in the middle of the play and he can't see some of the best passing options from that vantage point.

It also has to do with pressure. As a defenseman, he can see the pressure coming at him and can read his options more clearly. As a forward deep in the offensive zone he has to earn his space with the puck, and he has to do more with the puck with less ice.

As a defenseman, his skating ability was better highlighted as well. He picked up pucks in the corner with speed well and was able to beat fore-checkers with his feet.

He was always very responsible defensively, and as a center he played in his fair share of defensive corners, so he was good one-on-one and had a functional knowledge of pinning and containment.

Long-term, as a forward with limited offensive upside, his prospects of moving forward in hockey were not very encouraging. As a smooth skating defenseman who was responsible in his own end and an outstanding passer, his upside seemed untapped.

It was clear that we had found two kids who were playing out of position. Once we made the change our team was much stronger and the kids themselves were able to show their strengths more consistently.

COACHING CHALLENGE #22: PLAYERS WHO CAN PLAY MULTIPLE POSITIONS

1. How many of your players do you know can play multiple positions?
2. List three ways you can determine if players are playing in the position that gives them the best chance to be successful.
3. List three ways you can help all of your players become comfortable playing a second position.

23

THE CHICKEN OR THE EGG

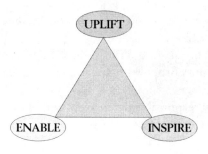

STRATEGY #23: INSPIRE BY SHOWING CONFIDENCE FIRST.

Be on the lookout for ways to show confidence in your players; you never know how they will reward your faith.

WE WERE PLAYING in a very physical game on the road in a rink that was difficult to get wins. Generally, when we went into this rink we had to prepare for a very tight checking and hard-hitting game. We had played very well in this rink this season; it was our third trip in and it played very similarly to the two before.

Late in the second period, Zack hurt his shoulder in an open ice collision. It wasn't serious enough to keep him out of the line-up in future games, but was tender so we decided to keep him out of the rest of this game.

Zack had been playing well of late with AJ and Cain so I was undecided regarding who would take his spot. I motioned for Matt to come back up to forward for the rest of the game to make three lines, but I didn't know who to put in Zack's spot.

The next time AJ's line came up I was ready to send Matt out on the wing with AJ and Cain when Bud said, "Robbie you're up with AJ and Cain!"

I was surprised, I wasn't even thinking about Robbie and here was Bud just sending him out there. I gave Bud a look and he just smiled back at me as Robbie jumped the boards to take his shift.

The opportunity brought Robbie out of his shell. He went on to score two third period goals and we went on to win the game 3-1, both of which were of the highlight variety, showing skills and confidence that we had no idea that he had. We knew he was a good player and we knew that he had potential, but we also thought he would take a while to develop.

His play was so surprising, Bubba yelled down the bench "Who's the new guy?"

It was amazing to watch this player take one opportunity and run with it like that. His energy, his drive and determination to make plays were like nothing we'd seen before from him. He played with passion and courage as he drove the net with the puck. That performance is one that we will remember for a long time.

After the game, there was no question that Forrest would give Robbie the work boots. The work boots was a symbol of the hardest working player on our team. We awarded the boots to the player who worked the hardest and was the best team player. The winner of the work boots signs them with a sharpie, wears them out of the arena and carries them in his bag until the next game, where he picks the next winner.

This was Robbie's first time winning them. He was beaming with pride as Forrest presented them to him. Everyone was so happy for him. He is such a laid-back person, who is so respectful to his teammates; we didn't know it was in him to play that way.

As he was leaving the locker room, Bud and I pulled him aside to talk to him.

I asked him, "Wow Robbie, where did that come from?"

He just smiled and said, "I couldn't let Bud down after he gave me that chance. I just wanted to show him how appreciative I was that he showed confidence in me like that."

Stunned at his response, I just said, "Well, can we expect that kind of play from now on?"

"Yep!" he said, as he left the locker room.

I was quiet all the way home, Bud knew I was trying to absorb what just happened. Why did this player all of sudden play to his capability, when to this point he rarely showed glimpses?

I turned to Bud and asked him, "How did you know he was going to play like that?"

Bud said, "I didn't know, I just had a gut feeling."

Sometimes when a coach unexpectedly shows confidence in a player it transfers directly to the player's perception of himself and he goes out and performs to the utmost of his ability. He believes because you believe. I think that's what happened with Robbie tonight.

It truly is a chicken and the egg situation relative to confidence. What comes first, confidence in his ability or you as the coach showing confidence in his ability? If the player lacks confidence and you never make him feel that you believe in him, how is he supposed to get it?

Players build confidence through a series of successes. Those little victories expand how they view themselves. When a coach shows faith in a player in a critical situation, he is creating a success opportunity for the player, who feels obligated to go out and prove the coach right.

I learned a valuable lesson that night. Showing confidence in players is one of the best ways to UPLIFT, ENABLE and INSPIRE them to realize their potential.

Robbie hadn't been the same player since. He had taken off rapidly. We were constantly looking for opportunities to show faith in him both in practice and in the games. What had been interesting was that in practice we saw Robbie at the front of the line which had never been the case before. The experience has made me a better coach and I was able to feel the wonderful feeling of watching that player succeed.

I think Bud knew all along.

COACHING CHALLENGE #23: SHOW CONFIDENCE IN YOUR PLAYERS

1. Identify a player on your team who doesn't play with much confidence. Describe three ways you can show confidence in him.
2. List the key situations in a hockey game that you can reward your players by displaying confidence in them.
3. What situations from the list you created can you look to use the player you identified in question #1 that he knows you are showing confidence in him?
4. Describe a way you can manufacture an important moment to which you inspire the player to perform knowing you are showing confidence in him.
5. How can you reinforce the importance this player has on your team?

24

TRIANGLE HOCKEY

STRATEGY #24: USE TRIANGLES TO TEACH OFFENSIVE AWARENESS.

Offensive hockey is all about triangles. Teach your players to understand and manipulate triangles and you teach them offensive support.

IT WAS THE second week in November and while the team was performing well, I was excited to see another Coaching Seminar on the schedule later in the week. I had learned and applied so much from the first two; three speeds of hockey and multi-tasking. I couldn't wait to find out what the third would be and how I could apply it to our team.

John welcomed us to the seminar and revealed that the topic this month would be Triangle Hockey.

He described triangle hockey as a team play structure that would teach young players how to read the play offensively and move purposefully in all areas of the ice, with and without the puck.

John said hockey coaches take criticism because there is a fine line between structure and creativity. How much team structure can you have on a team before you cripple individual creativity? Coaches tend to err on the side of structure and use five man systems to teach the tactical aspect of the game. For years, rigid and over-structured team play systems have produced a generation of players who lack offensive skill and creativity.

Triangle hockey is a team play structure but the difference is it relies on the creativity of the players to be successful. The difference between triangle hockey and our conventional team play structures is that the triangle is governed only by a single set of principles, applied in all areas of the ice. From a coaching perspective, if you teach triangle hockey, you don't need to have a separate system for each part of the game; breakout, fore-check, power play, neutral zone offense, transition offense, etc. You simply teach your players how to manipulate the triangle in all areas of the ice as your universal team play structure, then spend the rest of your time developing the players' individual skills, tactics, and read-and-react response ability.

The triangle bridges individual skills with team play. It is a simplistic system of play model designed to guide decision-making, creating automated responses from all players on the ice while promoting creativity.

Our players need to understand that once they step on the ice every move they make has a tactical implication. The triangle teaches them to identify their role in the play and they can react in support. Many players have a great individual skill base but have difficulty reading their role in certain situations.

The best part of triangle hockey is that it is very easy to teach and players of all ages are able to understand and apply the principles and tactics in all game situations.

Look at how it works:

Four universal principles govern triangle hockey.

1. Triangulation
   - Wherever the puck is we need to create two triangles: a primary triangle at the puck and a secondary or transition triangle away from the puck where one player is always a link between both triangles.

Figure 9:

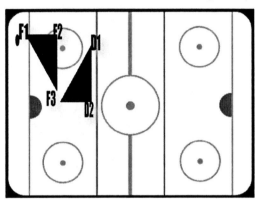

F1, F2 and F3 is the primary triangle

D1, D2 and F3 is the transition triangle

2. Support
   - We want to position our triangle so it always has support on two sides of the puck. This is called L-Support. This ensures the puck carrier always has two passing options with the puck positioned at the point of the L.

Figure 10:

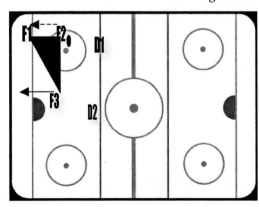

When F2 has the puck L-Support is achieved.

If he passes to F1, F3 must move to maintain the L.

■ ■ ■

3. Numerical Advantage
   - Offensively we want to create two-on-ones all over the ice. Our goal is to manipulate the triangle to isolate and outnumber defenders.

Figure 11:

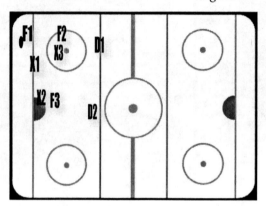

Right now it is 3 on 3 down low, the offensive team F1, F2, and F3 must rotate their position to create a 2 on 1 against X1, X2 and X3.

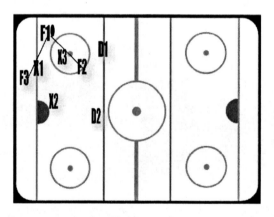

By rotating their positioning the F's are able to create momentary 2 on 1's and force the defense (X's) to adjust.

■ ■ ■

4. Transition
   - One player always links the two triangles and is always positioned in both a strong offensive position and defensive position at the same time.

Figure 12:

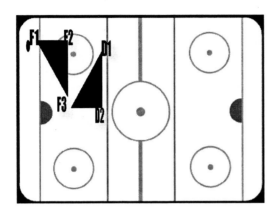

F3 is a part of both the primary offensive triangle (F1, F2 and F3) and the transition triangle (D1, D2 and F3). He is in a great offensive position but he is also in an excellent defensive position at the same time.

One player must be in this position, while it's not the same player, we must rotate someone into this linking position all the time.

John went on to explain how it relates to our program.

"The advantage of teaching triangle hockey to players in our system is the universal application and rotation principles of the triangle. This will make our teams very adaptable and provide much more opportunity for us as coaches to make in-game adjustments without having to teach multiple systems."

"The best example of this is the fore-check, let's say your team likes an aggressive 2-1-2 fore-checking system, but you are now protecting a lead late in the game, what do you do? Well if you have taught a 1-2-2 that gives you the option of changing your system to the more conservative fore-check to protect the lead. If your team understood triangles all you would have to do is rotate the primary triangle to change the system. By teaching the principles that guide the movement of triangles you save a ton of time in teaching five man systems, time which can now be used to develop the skill base of the player."

Figure 13:

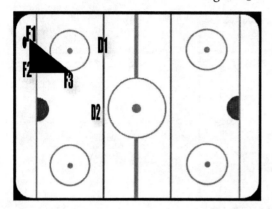

2-1-2 Fore-check triangle

Figure 15:

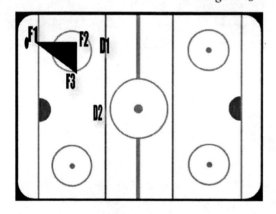

1-2-2 Fore-check triangle

** By rotating the triangle we are able to shift immediately into a more conservative fore-checking system.

After hearing John's presentation, I began to look at Triangle hockey from our team's perspective.

Triangle hockey was exactly what we needed; there were a couple instances in the season to this point when we changed from an aggressive fore-check to a passive fore-check to protect a lead. We hadn't spent any time developing a conservative fore-checking system to this point; our players would eventually back off and in some cases literally stand around. They didn't understand how to use a conservative fore-check to force turnovers in the neutral zone and counter attack. Our staff was fully prepared to just teach a separate system, but now I was leaning towards teaching triangles.

In John's presentation, he used video to show how common triangles are in every system. He had prepared a complete drill manual to help us implement triangle hockey into our season and teach the kids the principles and movement of the triangle. I found the drill manual helpful, but I also decided to ask John if I could use his video to help our players understand what we were trying to do.

Of course, John not only gave me the video to use, but also offered to help with the presentation to the players. All I could think about was how good a team I would have if the Atom coaches had taught triangle hockey to these players, and our team had two years of experience using this structure. I could only imagine how versatile our team would be at this stage with all that time using the structure under their belt.

COACHING CHALLENGE #24: UNDERSTANDING TRIANGLE HOCKEY

1. Draw any team play system. At the point of the puck, what shape is the basic support positioning?
2. What happens if the puck changes sides, how do your players rotate?
3. Take your team play systems that you drew previously, rotate the triangle at the point of the puck, and see what happens.

If we use triangles in every team play system, why limit our players to knowledge of just that system, when you teach triangle hockey, our players would know the principles of movement that would allow them to play any system thereafter?

25

VIDEO AS A TEACHING TOOL

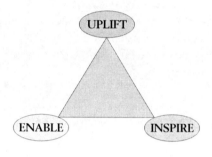

STRATEGY #25: USE VIDEO AS A TEACHING TOOL.

A picture is worth a thousand words.

AFTER WITNESSING JOHN'S masterful use of video to help teach our players triangle hockey, I couldn't believe how much the visual example fast-forwarded the learning process. I knew that 'a picture was worth a thousand words' but I never thought using video would have this impact. It gave me a great idea.

We had just finished our midseason assessments and had conducted one-on-one progress meetings with the players. Much of the focus was on the improvement the player had made to that point in the season and a continual emphasis was on finding ways for the player to play to his strengths.

Now that I had seen the video work, I decided to tape the next eight games of the season and from that tape create a video profile of our team. I wanted to capture the moments of perfect execution in all phases of the game, a highlight tape of us at our best. Then I wanted to take a couple players and create a video profile of them, a video collage of them performing at their best.

I wanted to see if the video profile would help the player identify with his strengths more because the video was actually of them. I also wondered how showing a player positive video of himself would help in his preparation for games, especially in the area of positive visualization.

I picked Brock, Adam, Carter and Ricky as our video profile subjects. I had a plan for each player and was on the lookout for clips I wanted to capture.

For Brock, I wanted to reign in his focus. He was a player who tried to do too much and many times would get caught over-handling the puck when he should make a play and under-handling the puck when he should try to create something. He was a very tough player to play with because you never knew what he was going to do.

For Adam, I wanted to show him the power aspect of his game. He had so much potential to dominate the play down low, but I found he still fell into his bad habits of trying to finesse everyone.

I was excited to show Carter some opportunities where he could be active away from the puck. He had made great strides to this point and I thought the video could only help. I also wanted a shot profile of Ricky so Tony could show him areas where he could improve his rebound control on the first shot.

I started with Brock. I pulled all of his shifts for six games and put them on one disk so I could properly analyze what he was doing.

I then took all the good things that he did and collected them separately along with a few instances that we wanted him to make changes.

The biggest area of improvement that Brock had to make in his game was that he sometimes over-estimated his ability, to the point where it caused him to make very poor decisions. For example, he would engage one-on-one from anywhere on the ice with a success rate of under 10%. I felt there were times when he should have gone one-on-one, but I would have liked to see him work for space and to isolate defenders into two-on-ones.

When Brock gets the puck, he goes right at someone and it costs him and his line-mates many chances to score. To illustrate this point, I showed him a clip of where he had time to draw the defender to him and open up a passing lane and space for Robbie who would have a better angle at the net. I then showed him an instance where he took his time and made a great play. There was one clip where he worked a give and go with Reese and he scored a goal. The pass he made to Reese drew the defender to Reese who gave Brock the puck back with an unobstructed lane to the net.

Then I followed those clips with instances where Brock tried to force one-on-ones. After two or three clips Brock said, "What was I thinking?" Acknowledging that he had an adjustment to make, as soon as he saw for himself, he was ready to learn so I stopped the video.

We then engaged in a wonderful discussion about his approach, his use of space, and his decision making with the puck. He actually went back in the tape to tell me what he should do the next time. It was really positive, I felt like he had made a break-through.

I felt the key was not to focus on the mistake, but rather to encourage Brock to look for options and his use of space to make good decisions. I didn't want him to feel that I was using the video to badger him about his play. I felt if I kept it positive and showed some good clips as well, he would appreciate my intentions.

The one thing about Brock was that he loves to play hockey and he has an intense desire to be good at it. For the first time this year, I felt I was making some headway with him. He understood what I was trying to do.

I think to this point he had been resistant because he was afraid I was trying to take the puck out of his hands. Whenever I talked to him about his decision-making, he interpreted that I was not confident in his ability with the puck. He took those discussions as a challenge to prove that he could beat the guy one-on-one, which led to occasions when he forced the play more and more. We were moving in opposite directions. The video was a way to get him to see what I saw and that made all the difference.

In his very next game he made two really nice 'give and go' type plays. His movement without the puck was much improved, and while he still had a long way to go, he was making adjustments. I pulled the good plays off the game tape and showed it to him the next day; he was excited. For the first time I think he knew I was taking an interest in him to help him.

With so much early success in using the video with Brock, I moved on to Adam and Carter. Both players are intelligent people, so they were very interactive and loved to watch the video. Adam even noticed that Forrest was always setting little screens in the offensive zone, and Adam hadn't recognized it on the ice. He said he'd be looking for that in the games to take better advantage.

When Carter viewed the video he was shocked at how much standing around he was doing. At one point he was talking to the screen, "Move!" he yelled at himself. "Why am I not moving?"

"That's exactly what I'm thinking when the game is going on," I said jokingly.

Carter had made great strides with his play without the puck. He saw where his opportunities presented themselves and he was another player who really benefited from seeing himself in action.

The next player was Ricky.

When Tony and I watched Ricky on video, we didn't realize how many rebounds he gave out. However, the more we watched the video the more we saw Ricky turn his crease area into a rebound heaven for goal scorers. He left too many first shot pucks five to seven feet away from his body.

We logged the number of second chance opportunities that he was giving up for three games.

Tony was getting agitated as he logged notes on second chance after second chance. I asked him, "Is there anything we can do to help his rebound control? This is getting ridiculous."

"Absolutely, Ricky is playing goal like a 'V' when he should be playing goal like a 'U'," he said.

"What's the difference?" I asked confused. "I've heard of butterfly, stand-up, Quebec style and hybrid style goalies, but I've never heard of anyone say 'V' or 'U' style," I said thinking aloud.

Tony began to explain. "It's not a style thing; every goalie has a unique style. You could classify goalies into certain genre's, which is what butterfly, stand up, and hybrid is. That is more of a classification for comparison and modeling purposes. Ricky's problem is his mental approach to the first shot."

"It is obvious that his mental approach to the first shot is that he is satisfied just stopping the puck. He really has no regard or plan for the puck once he stops it. It is clear that he believes that his job is to stop the first puck in whatever way that he can. Therefore, he is playing like a 'V'. The letter 'V' is an easy way to describe the deflecting approach to the first shot."

"Now when a goalie approaches the first shot like the letter 'U' it means instead of deflecting pucks, a 'U' goalie would prefer to gather them in like a funnel. A 'U' goalie relies on his ability to get square to the puck so that the first shot will come to him, instead of the goalie reaching for the puck."

"This is a very important distinction because if you are a 'V' you don't mind getting extended and reaching to make saves because as long as you stop the first puck, you are happy. When you are a 'U', it's the exact opposite; you don't get extended unless you have to. When a goalie reaches to make a save, he is essentially punching at the puck, not knowing where it will go. When you are square to the puck, the puck tends to come to you and therefore you are more likely to suck it into the core of your body."

"We need to get Ricky to use his feet more effectively to get square to the first puck, and save his reaching and scrambling ability to make any cross crease type of saves."

"The part of Ricky's game that just screams for attention when you watch the video is that he reaches for almost every puck. He rarely makes a 'routine' save. Once he sees the video I'm sure he'll agree that we have some work to do."

We brought Ricky in to practice a little early so Tony and I could review the video with him. We decided to allow him to watch the first game through without saying anything to him. Then after watching the game, we asked him if he had any impressions on what he saw.

He, too, was surprised at how he was playing some easy saves; he realized he was making it more difficult than it needed to be. He was also disappointed in himself on a couple of goals against.

"Instead of working on deflecting pucks to the corner in practice, let's try to gather everything in to see if it makes a difference in your rebound control. Let's just focus on getting square to the first shot and controlling the puck. I think if you do that you will not only reduce the number of rebounds you give in a game, you will be more in control of the game. What do you think?" Tony suggested.

"Yeah, I want to try it. I look like I'm making things more difficult than they really are," Ricky said knowingly.

Tony asked me to structure a couple shooting drills where the shot came from a predictable angle and so he could work with Ricky to get square to the puck and pull shots into him instead of pushing them away.

Initially, Ricky found the root of the problem. He just couldn't get square to the puck on the right angle. I gave him a lot of credit; he worked at it and in time was able to show signs of improvement.

Tony decided to video practices as well so he could monitor Ricky's progress more frequently and Tony and I worked together to design specific drills in practice for the goalie's development.

I had Tony hooked on video analysis and Ricky was a sponge. He was rushing to change after practice to spend five minutes with Tony watching certain drills and it became a ritual for them.

Tony then decided to take the same approach with Blake.

What was interesting was we were getting to a point where we would have two different goalie development drills, one for Ricky to get square to the puck, which is an area Blake excels. The other drill was for Blake to work on his quick feet in the crease area, which was an area that Ricky excelled. The two goalies realized that weakness of one was the strength of the other and they started working together. Then the two of them were starting to watch the video together and it was making a tremendous difference in each of their games.

Instead of our goalies working to compete with each other, they worked together to push each other. It was very different than what either of them had experienced in the past. Usually tension between goalies is generally the first area where a team's chemistry breaks down. On our team, these guys were pushing each other really hard but they were working together. It was great for the whole team to see.

Video analysis changed our goaltenders in so many positive ways that it was tough to pinpoint what the biggest value was. However when I thought about it, the biggest benefit was how hard they pushed each other in practice. It was fun to watch.

COACHING CHALLENGE #25: USING VIDEO AS A TEACHING TOOL

1. If video is the best visual feedback a player has to assess his own play, how can you utilize it?
2. List three people that you know right now that you could ask to video games.
3. Is there anyone on or around your team with access to digital video and editing programs?
4. Name one situation for which you wish you had video as a tool to illustrate your teaching point.

26

Sport Specific Training

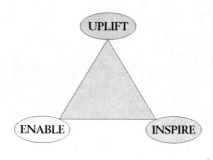

STRATEGY #26: DEVELOP OFF-ICE PREPARATION AND TRAINING HABITS.

Link off-ice work habits to on-ice performance.

IT WAS CLOSE to the halfway point in our season and we had a break in the schedule, so it was a good time to dedicate a practice to re-test.

After the re-test, I compared my notes from the preseason testing to look for improvements from all the players, but there were a couple red flags.

I was concerned with the core strength testing scores of Teddy, Adam and Bubba. Each of them had assured me that they had been working on the exercises prescribed to improve their strength.

I wanted to see how many of our players would have their recovery times in the ideal range. We only had one player in the ideal range from the first test, but having had half a season under their belt and the recommended remedial bike and sprint work, it was going to be interesting to see how much of an improvement they were able to make.

The two notables were Zack and Brock, I felt that both had made gains, but I was curious to see how many teammates they would overtake.

After the testing was complete Bud, Tony and I were anxious to compare the results.

The aspect that was most impressive was every player had improved his scores in every category. It was clear to me the work they had done away from the rink and the work we did during practice had worked. The numbers spoke volumes and I don't think any of us were expecting that. I think we were all expecting to see someone fall off, but to our surprise, no one did. That was exciting.

AJ continued to lead the way; this time expanding his dominance over all players on the team. He posted the best time in every test. He overtook Robbie for the team lead in the skating agility with a puck test. The improvement in his ability to carry speed in the corners was unreal. All the players on the team actually made big gains in the skating agility test. When I watched the tape of the tests again, the biggest improvement was each player's ability to carry speed in the turns. Each player had developed a stop-turn change of direction skill which helped them change direction 180 degrees without coming to a complete stop or widening the turning radius.

Zack shot up the standings to post the third best recovery time on the team. What was most impressive was he also ranked in the top five in speed for the two times. His ability to blend performance with recovery was amazing compared to where he started.

I asked him how he made such gains in his recovery and his answer was very interesting. He attributed his improvement to the program. His program called for a lot of plyometric-type training, quick feet and agility drills, interval sprint work both on the bike and on the track. What was interesting was the amount of work he did on his balance. He dedicated significant time in his training to using unstable surfaces such as wobble boards and balls.

In talking to him, he thought his biggest improvement came from the gains he had made in his balance. I found that to be very interesting. He said that after a few weeks of working on unstable surfaces and utilizing training movements that were more hockey-specific he was able to find his balance and that made a big difference in his training.

He also dedicated his energy to work on his core, with a big emphasis on his lower back strength, which he said helped him in all areas of his training.

While he was the player with the most to gain because of his starting point, he certainly made up a ton of ground and rated in the top half in each of the tests.

After seeing his test results, he was so inspired to continue with his training. He knew he was improving because he would periodically retest himself.

However, with the formal test results he was able to see how much ground he gained on his teammates, and he became even more motivated.

The key with Zack was to be on a proper program. Not to just join a gym and fool around with the machines, or follow someone else's program. He was on a program that was sport specific and addressed his personal needs as an athlete. Based on the results of his testing, he would now create new fitness goals for himself and to help meet his objectives he would alter his program, routines and exercises accordingly.

The advancements in strength and conditioning training continue to evolve at an unbelievable rate. What was the fitness rage five years ago had reinvented and expanded a thousand times over. Getting into sport-specific condition has never been more important. Players work hard on their fitness and strength levels year round, and the off-season focus is quickly becoming the norm.

I felt fortunate that I was able to use Coach Stone and his resources to help our players focus on the right areas of fitness, and to develop a personal training program with specific goals and objectives. However, having spoken to many players both at the University and around the rink, the information was continuing to evolve and the amount of quality information was starting to make its way to the mainstream.

The internet presents many innovative training techniques, testing structures and other great information. There are even on-line fitness consultants from every sport available to work with players if there is no one to help them in their area. In some of the bigger cities, there are hockey specific training gyms, where the entire customer base is hockey players.

I couldn't wait to take our players into a gym near us that was hockey specific. I was looking forward to seeing our players work directly with other hockey players and learn first hand what it takes from a physical fitness perspective to compete at the various levels of the sport.

We scheduled meetings with each of the families again to share the results, provide additional resources and to encourage each of our players to continue to put the time and effort into working on their strength and conditioning off ice.

I was counting on these improvements to be a competitive advantage for us when we hit the playoffs. If our players were able to make these gains in four months, what would they be like after another two or three months of training?

COACHING CHALLENGE #26: SPORT SPECIFIC TRAINING

1. How many of your players are on a personalized hockey strength and conditioning program?
2. Who are the hockey fitness leaders in your community that could help your team?
3. What can you, as the coach, do to create a personal best program for your athletes, allowing them to track their progress through testing?
4. Who are the high performing hockey players in your community? Would any of them be interested in working out with your team, so your players can see first hand what a quality workout looks like?

27

SOMETIMES THE BEST SKILL IS A SHORT MEMORY

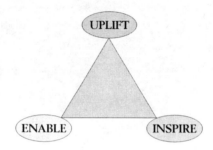

STRATEGY #27: MONITOR YOUR PLAYERS' INTERNAL DIALOGUE

Focus is about staying in the moment. Work hard to keep your players' attention to the
<u>now</u>, not what was.

THE GAME WAS well under way and it was obvious that our opponent had great respect for our team speed. Their defense strategy was one we hadn't faced to this point in the season and through the first period our team looked confused.

Our defense was not used to the extra time and space in our own zone. On a couple of occasions in the first period, they dumped the puck in and their first fore-checker was standing at the top of the circles. Sammy went back once to get a dump in and stopped behind the net, and all five of their players were in the neutral zone.

During the period we tried to make some adjustments, we asked our defense to take their time and give us a chance to run a counter play. We found that we were just racing back up the ice into the trap, often moving the puck too soon and making it much easier on them to create turnovers. It was the worst first period of hockey that we had played all year where we didn't generate any notable chances to score.

For the second period, we made an adjustment where one defense would carry the puck up one side of the ice while the other defense slipped in behind him. When the first fore-checker moved to pressure our puck carrier at the blue-line, he would pass the puck back to his partner who would swing the puck to the opposite side of the ice. We knew if we could get the trap to commit to one side of the ice and quickly change the point of attack, we would go a long way to breaking it.

In the first shift of the second period, Sammy gathered the dump in, stopped behind the net, waited for his teammates to get into position and then started up the left side of the ice. Cliff, who was his partner, was supposed to provide back support but instead he skated along side Sammy. When the fore check began to commit, Sammy attempted to pass to Cliff who was even with him, and the first fore-checker intercepted the pass and walked in on a breakaway, scoring the first goal of the game.

Cliff came back to the bench visibly upset. He positioned himself poorly to support Sammy and caused the turnover and he knew it. Bud let him vent a bit on the bench before he attempted to talk to him. In a situation like that, Bud did not need to point out the mistake; Cliff was the first to know. Bud's job was to try to get him ready for the next shift.

Bud bent down to Cliff's level, patted him on the back, and tried to reassure him that we would be 'ok' and to shake it off. Cliff nodded to tell Bud he understood, but we all knew he wasn't letting it go. He had dropped his head and was staring at his skates clearly beating himself up over his mental error.

"Come on Cliff, get your head up, you and Sammy are up next." Clearly, Bud was trying again to motivate him and clear his mind.

Cliff went on the ice looking for a hit. He had his eye on a developing play and tried to anticipate the pass to a player along the boards he had lined up. Cliff read the passer and tried to get a jump on the pass, but the pass didn't go there. Cliff had opened up a gap between him and Sammy and the passer hit a player cutting into that space.

Cliff was caught! It was a two-on-one against Sammy. Sammy did a great job to take away the pass, but the shooter was on his off-wing and was able to beat Dish with a great shot from just outside the hash marks. This time Cliff was beside himself. In two shifts, he had made two mistakes that led directly to goals.

We knew we were going to have an uphill battle. Anytime you are playing against a trapping team, you can't afford to let them play with the lead. The longer they play with the lead the harder it becomes to generate quality chances to score.

Our team was in a panic. We didn't respond well to the adversity. One mistake, led to another mistake, which now led us into our bad habits.

Our worst team habit was that we tended to get individual when we got down in the game. Everyone tried to be the hero, and against a trapping team, that was a recipe for disaster.

We started to come unraveled. First Cliff, then AJ tried to go one-on-two, then Brock tried to skate the puck through the neutral zone. Finally, Brownie over skated the puck and that led to the third goal.

Before we knew it, it was 4-0 late in the third.

Cliff never got his composure back, he took two undisciplined penalties late in the game, and we never had a chance.

AJ scored one goal with a minute to go in the game on a highlight reel individual effort, but it was much too late.

I went in the room after the game and said nothing about the game; I reminded them of practice the next day and decided to leave the team with their thoughts. This was a good time to let the game settle with them overnight and we'd address the game tomorrow at practice.

On the way home Bud, Tony and I discussed the game at length. Bud said that Cliff couldn't let go of his first mistake and he let it bother him and affect his play the remainder of the game. He wasn't able to mentally recover and refocus. He played in the past the entire second and third period.

Cliff is an emotional player, he plays the game with a great deal of passion, and he tends to swing with the momentum of the game. When things are going well, he excels, and when things start to go bad, his game deteriorates at the same pace. He plays on an emotional roller coaster.

Bud suggested that we pull him aside and tell him about "the next skill he needs to learn."

Tony asked, "What skill is that Bud?"

Bud smiled and replied, "A short memory."

At practice the next day, Bud pulled Cliff aside and spoke to him about learning to play in the present. Cliff had to learn from his mistakes, and find a better way to deal with the natural feelings of frustration and anger. This was going to be a tough adjustment for him. He takes a lot of pride in his game and puts a lot of pressure on himself to be a solid player every game.

To bring his game to the next level, he needed emotional control. He needed to learn how his emotions affected his game.

He is a player that when he makes one good play it usually leads to another good play. Conversely, one bad decision usually leads to another bad decision. He steps out of the context of the game to try to make up for his mistakes. This is where he lets himself down.

For Cliff to overcome this hurdle in his development his adjustment has to be in the way he talks to himself after every shift.

Bud asked him, "What do you think about when you come off after each shift?"

"I think about what I could have or should have done in whatever situations that came up in the shift," Cliff responded honestly.

"Well, if you are always thinking about what happened does it makes sense that you are playing the game in the past? Whatever happened in the past is directly affecting the way you play in the future," Bud said.

"Yeah, but how do you learn from your mistakes?" Cliff asked.

"Well I'm no expert, but I know that if you are thinking of negative things, you will attract more of the same, and if you are thinking positive things, you will tend to attract more of the same," Bud said in a riddle.

Cliff looked confused.

Bud continued, "Cliff, once the play is over, you can't do anything to change it. So how does dwelling on it in between shifts help you in your next shift?"

Cliff shrugged his shoulders.

"Here's what I think we need to do. We have three defense pairings so that means when you come off from a shift, there are two more shifts in between your next shift. In the first thirty seconds after you come off, think about the shift you just had. If we need to make adjustments or you need to vent in frustration, use that first thirty seconds. Then take the next thirty seconds to get ready for the next shift. Start to refocus on positive things, get yourself back in the game by thinking positive thoughts. Then go on the ice and execute with a clear mind," Bud finished watching Cliff closely to see if he was making any headway.

Cliff nodded his head and said, "I like that, I was getting worried that you were going to tell me that I needed to stay positive all the time. It's going to take me a while to change. I like this way better, because it allows me time to unwind from the previous shift before I start looking ahead."

"You aren't that good Cliff," Bud said smiling. "Cliff, I know you are an emotional player who is very good because of your passion, but we need to channel that emotion so it works for you. Right now, it is not working for you. It's working against you. In time we hope to shorten the amount of time you need to unwind or let the previous shift go. If needed, it will be just a moment of instruction and then you will move to thinking about the shift at hand. It might take some time, but at least we know where we are trying to go with this," Bud said trying to assure Cliff that we would get there.

"Thanks Bud," Cliff said with the utmost respect and appreciation.

COACHING CHALLENGE #27: TEACHING PLAYERS TO RE-FOCUS

Coaching kids who play with passion and take a pride in their game is tough. They tend to be like Cliff in that they ride the emotion of the game. It is hard to keep them focused on the next shift and to have a positive outlook each time they step on the ice.

1. Identify one player you either coach now or you have coached in the past who plays the game in the past. What steps should you take to help that player re-focus during the game?
2. Name three ways you can learn how players talk to themselves between shifts.
3. How can you find out how each player prepares for each shift?

28

PLAYING WITHOUT THE PUCK

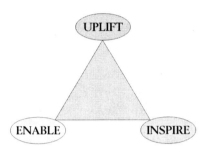

STRATEGY #28: ONE PLAYING FOR FOUR OR FOUR PLAYING FOR ONE?

Put a premium on players moving without the puck, reward players who move with a purpose.

WHEN I FIRST saw Carter play, he didn't play like a defenseman; he played like a fourth forward. It seemed like every time he touched the puck, he would take off with it. He didn't pass, he either worked himself into shooting position or he would attempt to pass when he ran out of room, or didn't have another play to make. It was obvious he had good skills, but he played a very limited game.

To see Carter sitting beside me watching game tape on the laptop and getting excited about joining a play without the puck was a sign of progress.

I had regularly scheduled meetings with Carter, fifteen minutes each practice that followed a game, to review game film. Carter was so receptive to the video; he was developing into quite a student of the game.

Carter was one of the initial four players we used video analysis as a teaching tool. He wasn't responding to rink board diagrams and walking him through practice. He made a couple adjustments but not nearly enough to get excited.

He turned the corner once we started breaking down game tape.

The biggest challenge for Carter was to move with a purpose when he didn't have the puck. Then when he got the puck, he would already be moving and would have an easier time reading the play. I wanted him to learn how to be dangerous on the weak-side of the ice. He needed to learn how to sneak into passing lanes, to provide back support for his partner and to create odd man situations by joining the rush at the right time.

It is tough to get most defensemen at this age to be an offensive presence. Most defensemen have been conditioned to just bang pucks off the boards when they get it, and haven't really developed good puck skills to use their partner and make good passes. Carter had an excellent offensive skill base; he just needed to learn how to be a factor in the play more consistently.

My development plan for Carter was to help him acquire four tactical skills. These skills would go a long way to help him become an offensive defenseman.

1. When defending at the puck, play for body control not puck possession.
   - When Carter would defend, he was totally focused on stealing the puck. Many times he would get beat one-on-one because he was playing the puck. I wanted him to focus on angling, body position, gap control, containment and pinning the puck carrier, and forget about the puck. His job was to pin the puck carrier and create a loose puck for a teammate.

Figure 15:

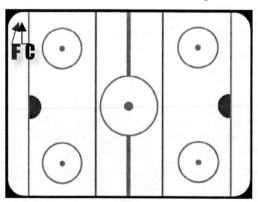

Carter is the C – in one on one situations, he must focus on establishing good defensive side position, reduce time and space, control the forward with his stick and move in for the pin.

2. When defending away from the puck, anticipate changes of possession and work hard to be a passing option.
   - When Carter is not directly involved in the play, he needs to support the play offensively by reading changes of possession and moving quickly to good areas of the ice where he can receive the pass.
   - If he makes himself available for passes when he is away from the puck, when he catches those passes he will have more room to skate it and make decisions

Figure 16:

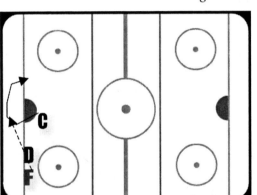

Carter is holding the front of the net, reads change of puck possession, and makes himself available for the pass.

3. Learn to join every play offensively from the weak-side.
   - If we break the play up one side of the ice, he needs to jump into that rush as either the third wave of attack or to create an odd man rush situation.
   - The play we were focusing on was a breakout from defensive zone coverage in the corner. Many times the center is defending down low and when the play breaks out he is in a poor position to join the rush. But the defenseman in front of the net is in a great position to join the rush and turn a one-on-one into a two-on-one or a two-on-two into a three-on-two.

Figure 17:

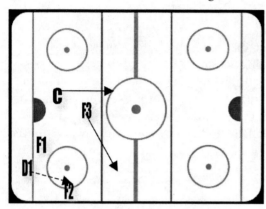

On a breakout when he is away from the puck he is in a better position to join the rush than F1 who is helping out down low. Carter can join the play with F2 and F3.

If their defenseman pinches at the point down on F2 Carter can turn a 1 on 1 into a 2 on 1 with F3.

◾ ◾ ◾

4. Learn to look to pass to his partner.
   - When Carter does get the puck, he tends to just force the play up ice, when he could just use his partner. By changing the point of attack it frees him up to join the rush from the weak-side which makes him much more dangerous.

Figure 18:

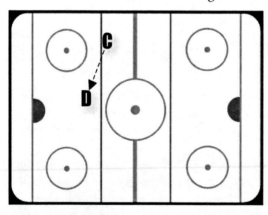

Carter has the puck in the neutral zone but he is outside the dots and has very little room to skate, he could pass to his partner who is in a much better position to see the ice and make a play. Carter could make the pass and read for an opportunity to join the rush on the weak side.

◾ ◾ ◾

I found the easiest of the four for him to incorporate into his game was joining the rush from the weak-side (#3) and the hardest habit to break was focusing on being a defender at the puck (#1). There are still times I think he could use his partner more (#4), but it's going to take a while to change his mind-set. Any gains he can make in these four areas will make him more noticeable and effective.

The video allowed him to see himself skating the puck into bad areas when there were chances to move the puck to his partner. He was also able to see himself fishing with his stick for the puck in the corner when he should be focusing on taking the man. The visual of seeing himself in action made all the difference. The video didn't lie and it was great to see him take ownership of his game and get committed to making the necessary changes.

I also taped an NHL game and pulled New Jersey's Scott Niedermayer's shifts so Carter could see how Scott was able to use his skating away from the puck to create so much on offense. Carter had identified Scott Niedermayer as a role model for his game, so to be able to show video evidence of Scott doing what we wanted Carter to do gave us so much more credibility with Carter. It became a great source of inspiration for him.

I told Carter a story about the first time I went to see Brett Hull play. "I was so excited to see Brett play that year, he was marching his way to seventy goals, and I couldn't wait to see him dominate the game."

"I remember being so disappointed. I thought Brett was going to do all these amazing end-to-end rushes and attack defensemen one-on-one and he didn't do any of that. He finished the game scoring two goals and adding an assist, but he lost a fan in me. I couldn't appreciate his offensive ability because I just assumed he would have the puck on his stick all the time. That's not the type of player Brett Hull is, he is so good because he plays so well without the puck. He finds seams in the offensive zone, he has a great sense of anticipation and timing and he is always ready to shoot."

"In the game I watched, the two goals he scored were both one-timer type shots from the high slot, both on passes from Adam Oates. I went into the game a fan of Brett Hull and left as an Adam Oates fan, because I could see Adam had the puck on his stick a lot more."

"Now of course, I see the game differently and have much more of an appreciation for Brett Hull's ability to play without the puck offensively."

I wanted Carter to see that so much of the game is without the puck and that it will be his ability to play without the puck that will give him more chances to play with it.

COACHING CHALLENGE #28: OFFENSIVE HOCKEY WITHOUT THE PUCK

1. Take a winger on your team, name three things you can teach him to do when he doesn't have the puck that would help him contribute to the offense more effectively.
2. Draw a drill that you could implement in practice that would help him recognize the reads and timing.
3. Other than video, what other tool could you use to help the player better understand the three tactics you want him to build into his game when he doesn't have the puck?

29

REWARD EFFORT

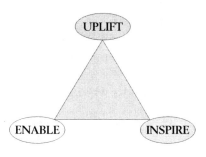

STRATEGY #29: REWARD EFFORT AND DETERMINATION

When you challenge a player and notice improvement in the effort and concentration put forth, make a point to encourage and reward.

I GOT A call from our A team coach Richard Black, who suggested it was time that I make a point to come and watch Kyle play. I had been calling Coach Black regularly through the season to get updates and progress reports on a few players including Kyle. We had had both Kyle and Kelsey out to a few of our practices since the season started and while both worked hard when they were out, I wasn't sure how accurate a practice was to gauge their progress. We hadn't had an opportunity, through suspension or injury of anyone on our team, to get them into any of our games to this point. It was important that we keep them practicing with us and had regular contact with Coach Black to keep up to date on their progress.

Coach Black called me to let me know that Kyle had made great strides recently in adjusting his game and thought it was a good time to get our thoughts. He said that Kyle had been working very hard to improve his foot speed and felt like there was visible progress that we should see.

One of the dangers when you have a player like Kyle, who has played on the AAA team for many years and is then sent to play with the A team is that he probably won't have to change his game much to be successful at the A level. The difference between AAA and A is generally speed, and while Kyle's foot speed is slow for the AAA level, he will likely have top end speed in the A division. The challenge is to avoid the trap of being complacent in his development because he is experiencing success at the A level. We wanted him to capitalize on the slower speed of the game to build confidence and use the confidence to help him compete for a spot on our team in the future.

I took Tony with me to watch the game, because I wanted him to watch Chad who was going to be the goalie that night. Coach Black said that Chad was asserting himself as the top goalie on his team and with him scheduled to start it was a great opportunity for us to "kill two birds with one stone."

Before the season started, Coach Black and I had many conversations concerning Kyle's development. We were wrestling with what position he should play on the A team. On our team he was probably a winger, but I didn't think Kyle should play wing on the A team. I felt if he really wanted to improve his skating, he should play center, that way he'd have full reign over the entire ice and thus more opportunity to skate in his games. Coach Black agreed and had been playing Kyle at center.

When we watched the first period of the game I was impressed with Kyle. He was always a hard working kid, but what jumped out at me was his skating. I found his acceleration was much improved and he was separating from the other players on the ice. I also noticed that he was carrying the puck more and trying to use his speed in the neutral zone. Kyle's play was noticeably different from his performance in August. Clearly, he had taken the right approach going to play with the A team. He was changing his game and it was noticeable.

Tony noticed that Kyle was creating a lot of scoring chances for himself, but his shot selection was very poor. There were a couple times when he was attacking the net and did not even attempt to move the goalie. He still used a wrist shot, which was fine but his release was slow and gave the goalie time to move and set for the shot. Tony suggested that we work with Kyle to develop a pull in snap shot, that way he would change the shooting angle slightly and give himself more net to shoot at. The pull-in snap shot would also go a long way to improving his release speed.

I thought that was a great idea, so we waited for Kyle after the game to give him some words of encouragement and to tell him and Coach Black our ideas about developing the pull-in snap shot.

Coach Black told Kyle we were waiting for him and Kyle made his way out to meet with us.

"Hi Kyle, you played a great game tonight," I started.

"Hi Coach, thanks very much," he said with a grin.

"Kyle, I wanted to tell you that I think your speed has improved in the last couple months so keep up the good work," I said encouragingly.

"Thanks Coach, I work on the exercises that you gave me after tryouts every night and I feel like they are helping me. Coach Black pushes me hard in practice. I also think that practicing with your team helps as well because I notice I am a lot faster out there," Kyle said.

"Coach Tony noticed something tonight with your shot that he'd like to tell you about," I said nodding to Tony.

"Yeah Kyle, I noticed that when you had some chances to shoot tonight you were hitting the goalie a lot. It almost looked like you were shooting right at him. The reason that happens is that the goalie is getting a good angle on your shot and you have to find a way to change the attack angle. What you need to do is develop a pull-in snapshot to change the shooting angle," Tony said as he motioned with his hands to simulate the shot.

"I've never heard of the pull-in snap shot before," Kyle said.

"Why don't you come to our next practice and Tony and I will show you. It's hard to show you properly here with an imaginary stick. Let's get on the ice and show you properly so you can start practicing it the right way," I said encouragingly.

"That sounds good," Kyle said excited. "Thanks for coming today."

"No problem, we'll see you at practice," I said.

We had specific shooting drills that we used as part of our goaltender development each practice. Generally, in that format Bud and I were able to float around and work on shooting technique with each player. During the first goalie development drill, I took a minute to show Kyle the pull-in snap shot technique and then asked Teddy to work with him as well. I found that kids responded really well to other kids, and Teddy was a good kid with an excellent pull-in snap shot.

Bud and I waited a month and then we dropped in to see Kyle and the A team play again.

Kyle continued to develop his foot speed, most notably his agility in small space situations. On a few occasions, he had attempted the pull-in snap shot which was also encouraging.

After watching the game, Bud and I both felt that if we needed Kyle to come up and play for us, he would be able to contribute. I felt that he was in position to compete for a spot on our team now. We needed to work with Coach Black to provide help and inspiration to Kelsey, who was not developing at a rate that would make him competitive for a spot on our team next year.

We decided to ask Coach Black if he would set up a meeting between Kelsey and us. We wanted to ask him exactly what his commitment was off-ice and if there was any other way we could help accelerate his improvement.

COACHING CHALLENGE #29: REWARD EFFORT AND DETERMINATION

1. What can you do to motivate and encourage a player who narrowly missed making your team?
2. What can you do to improve your relationship with the coach on the team that this player is playing on?
3. List all the reasons why it is important to continue to show interest and update yourself on this player's progress.

30

TIMING IS EVERYTHING

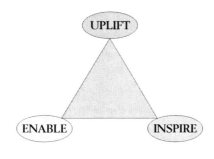

STRATEGY #30: TEACH TIMING AS A SKILL

Contact is a skill best utilized inside the context of the game. The best body checkers are able to recognize a great hit opportunity without having to hunt for it.

THERE WAS ONE game in particular that I thought was the turning point for Bubba. It was a game that he finally understood what we had been trying to teach him for the last three or four months. The breakthrough Bubba made that game was what he needed to springboard his game to the next level.

Bubba is a player who loves contact. He is a big, stocky kid who moves very well and you never have to ask him twice to finish his check. Where Bubba ran into trouble was that he had tunnel vision and it affected his ability to read other parts of the game. Essentially, he had shifts in which his total focus was to hunt someone and initiate contact.

Bubba had changed the momentum in a couple games with a single hit. He had provided a much-needed spark in some games, but in others, he had taken an ill-advised penalty, which cost us the game. The worst part about Bubba was that he had other skills, but when he locked into contact, all his other skills were thrown out the window and it was a shame. He just didn't understand that if he did certain things on the ice consistently, contact situations would present themselves. He shouldn't have to go looking for them.

I decided to use some game tape to show Bubba what I was talking about. I had isolated eight contacts, four of which he took penalties on and four of which were outstanding contacts.

In the four that he took penalties he was literally chasing the hit. He lined up the puck carrier and took a run. In the ones he had excellent contact, it happened within the context of the play and they had better impact and affect than the ones that he was chasing.

I showed him the clips one after the other and then asked him which hits he liked the best. He picked two hits that he liked, one was a player who was crossing in front of his partner and Bubba stepped up and caught him with his head down. The second one he liked was a pinching situation when he timed the contact perfect and it became a quality scoring chance for our team.

Then I asked him which ones he didn't like. He picked one hit that captured the essence of my point to him. He had taken a hit going back to get a dump in, and after the hit, the play went to the other corner. Bubba decided to race to the other corner and hit the new puck carrier, clearly out of frustration and retaliation from the hit he had just taken. Bubba was awarded a boarding penalty, which resulted in a goal against. I asked him what he didn't like about the hit.

"Well, I took a bad penalty and it cost us an important goal," he replied.

"After seeing these clips, I notice any time you chase a hit down, you take a penalty and it hurts the team. However, any time you hit in the context of the game not only is the hit more effective, but it is harder as well," I said starting to make my point.

"Yeah, a couple of those penalties were ugly, eh?" He said knowingly.

"Bubba, I like your physical play. I think you know that, but we need you on the ice and not in the penalty box. We have to find a way for you to play that allows you to be physical, but doesn't hurt the team or hurt someone else," I said.

"I know I have to stop chasing or hunting as Bud says," Bubba said acknowledging the problem.

"Here's the problem as I see it. You have to hit when the time is right. What is good timing?" I asked.

"It's when you hit at the right moment in the game," he answered.

"No, it's more than that. It is arriving at the right place, at the right time, with the right amount of speed. When you hunt for hits you don't have any of those, do you?" I asked.

"No, how do I get better timing?" He asked.

"Well instead of hunting, chasing and taking yourself out of the play for a hit, why don't you play your game and look for opportunities to make good contact?" I said.

"What do you mean by opportunities to make good contact?" He asked.

"Let's take a look at the hits that we liked and see if the answer is in those clips," I suggested.

When Bubba watched the clips, again he began to understand. At the end of our meeting, we decided on four good contact opportunities.

1. When the puck is slow to get to the winger and there is a good pinch opportunity.
2. When the puck carrier comes from the opposite side of the ice across the middle of the ice, there is a good opportunity to step up for contact.
3. When the puck carrier is on the rush and he tries to go wide, there is a good opportunity to pivot and step into the check.
4. When the opposing team likes to pass up the middle of the ice to the center-man on the breakout, which is a good chance to step up for contact.

Unless one of these situations occurs, Bubba is going to contain his check, play for pins and finish his check in the context of the game.

I was trying to impress upon Bubba that the opportunity for highlight reel checks only comes along a couple times during the game. He needs to focus on the skills that will make him a better hockey player. He needed to develop skills such as supporting his partner, making good outlet passes, taking away time and space from the puck carrier and his individual skills like improving his foot speed, developing a harder and more accurate shot.

It was time for him to play physical inside the context of the game. The good part of it was he now understood what Bud and I had been stressing. Bud and I were anxious to see how he would respond.

In one of the games, he didn't register one bone-crunching hit, but he was plus three with an assist on the winning goal. Another game, he caught a guy coming across the middle with an excellent open ice hit then he pinched down and finished his check creating a turnover that led to a goal.

He was turning it around slowly, but he would be a much more effective player in the long run.

COACHING CHALLENGE #30: TEACHING TIMING

1. In this chapter, we helped Bubba learn timing with respect to body contact. What other types of timing are important for players to learn?
2. List four drills that you have to improve timing.
3. Take one of the drills and shrink it and move it to a smaller area.

31

STUDENT-ATHLETES

STRATEGY #31: AN EDUCATION IS FOR LIFE

In the term 'student-athlete,' the student comes first. Take an interest and become an advocate of balanced living and academic achievement.

IT WAS A call I would have never expected. I was shocked, but at the same time I was very happy that Mrs. Carr, Sammy's mother, decided to call me.

Sammy wasn't doing very well at school. His grades had been slipping gradually for the last couple of years. It had reached a point where Mrs. Carr was concerned.

Education was very important to her and her husband. Sammy's sister just graduated high school with honours. She was receiving scholarship offers for her academics. Sammy showed academic potential, but to this point he had not applied himself.

Sammy was finishing his last year of middle school and his family was to the point where they needed to get his attention. Mrs. Carr suggested that she would like me to speak to Sammy to see if I could make a difference.

After speaking with Mrs. Carr, I decided to call Coach Stone at the university to hear his thoughts. I wanted to impress upon Sammy the importance of education without 'singing the same song his parents had been singing.'

Coach Stone asked about Sammy's academic history to be sure he was capable of higher grades and that he was choosing to be unapplied. I reassured him that Sammy came from an academic family and that he had shown capability both in the past, and in certain courses that he was taking currently.

Coach Stone suggested that our best approach was the student-athlete approach. We should model the US universities and create an academic eligibility for him in relation to the hockey team. Our task was to involve Sammy in creating an agreed minimum standard of academic performance to remain an active player on the hockey team.

Coach Stone offered to come in and talk to our entire team about the value of being good student-athletes early in their high school career. He thought we needed to address the whole team and emphasize the way good grades would expand their options as a hockey players. He felt that if we did it right there would be other families who would want to do the same thing that we were proposing to do with Sammy.

I called Mrs. Carr back and told her about our plan. First, we were going to schedule a seminar with Coach Stone for the entire team. Then we were going to meet with her family to create an academic eligibility program for Sammy. She was thrilled.

I was excited about the possibilities. As I continued to think of the potential impact that this could have, I figured it could also be a wonderful opportunity to educate our parents and players about the college hockey route.

Coach Stone walked into the meeting room where we had everyone assembled. He began to talk about college hockey in general. He asked a few questions to see how much everyone knew about college hockey, what it took to get there, and what it took to stay eligible.

It was very enlightening to me to hear Coach Stone talk about SAT's, GPA's, the NCAA (National Collegiate Athletic Association) Clearinghouse and academic eligibility. He went on to say that, NCAA programs only have 18 full hockey scholarships but carry a 22 to 25-man roster. Many players in the program are on some combination of hockey scholarship, financial aid and academic performance grants. It was very interesting to hear him break it down.

It surprised me to hear that Ivy League schools don't offer athletic scholarships; the scholarships are academic and most of the grants are based on financial need. That was an eye-opener. He went on to talk about the various leagues in the NCAA.

It became obvious that it was becoming harder to earn a full hockey scholarship and that many players needed to perform well academically in high school to qualify for a grant to cover the cost of their education.

He then presented case studies of student-athletes who went on to play pro hockey at all levels including teams in Europe. Then he had examples of student-athletes who went on to become professionals in other disciplines because of their education.

Coach Stone then said something interesting. He said, "I know a few of you guys are sitting there thinking, I'm going to the CHL (Canadian Hockey League) so I don't need to worry about all this. Well, let me leave you with this. Every year we recruit players from the CHL and while most of them have good study habits and are well prepared to perform academically in the school, there are also players who were not prepared for the rigors of university and therefore found themselves academically ineligible to play for the team. There would be nothing worse than playing four years in the CHL and having a CHL team prepared to pay for your education, only to find out that you can't handle the academics."

It was an outstanding presentation.

We then had a meeting scheduled with the Carr family to present Sammy with our plan for creating an academic eligibility standard for him.

I started the meeting by giving Sammy the opportunity to talk about his academic situation.

I then offered the floor to his parents who then expressed their concerns with his recent academic performance.

After hearing from them, I reiterated the highlights of Coach Stone's presentation about the importance of building good study habits and becoming a high performing student-athlete, with the student as the first priority.

Sammy acknowledged that he had been on cruise control in school as of late and agreed that he had more to give academically.

We then talked about his specific grades and I asked Sammy to assign a target grade to each class that he felt was well within range and a better reflection of what he was capable of achieving.

Once he assigned specific grades to each course and his parents agreed to his target grade, we then set a minimum standard of academic performance. As long as Sammy was above his minimum standard and pursuing his target grade, he would not miss any time. If he dipped below that minimum standard, he agreed to miss time with the team until the grade was improved. Sammy was to ask for help in terms of tutors, other supplemental academic help or time away from the team for academics if he felt he needed it.

We set it up in a contract form so he could sign it just to give the agreement an official feel from both his and his parents' perspective.

A couple days later, I received a call from Mrs. Carr and she proudly reported that Sammy's academic attitude had changed noticeably and she was thrilled that we were able to help. Our approach had helped to alleviate an on-going family battle. It turned out to be a win-win situation for everyone.

In the days that followed, I received calls from other families. They had heard about our approach with Sammy and wanted to talk about how their sons were applying themselves academically; they wanted to create similar academic performance goals linked to the hockey team.

What started as a phone call from a concerned mother turned into a complete program for our team. I couldn't be more grateful to Coach Stone who helped many parents ease their sons back on track.

The win we accomplished that day didn't show up in the standings, but it scored a ton of points for our program.

I was so excited I called John to let him in on the events and mentioned to him that Coach Stone had offered to speak to any team about combining athletics and academics.

Now I just hoped that Sammy and the other boys would follow through and we'd have some great success stories.

COACHING CHALLENGE #31: CREATING STUDENT-ATHLETES

1. As a coach, what can you do to help your players find a balance between athletics and academics?
2. What can you do to inspire your players to have the desire to excel in both academics and athletics?
3. How much of an impact do you have in the formation of your athletes' attitudes towards academic performance?

32

Sportsmanship

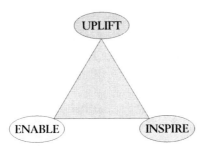

STRATEGY #32: GAME RESPECT STARTS WITH YOU COACH

Hold your players to a high standard of sportsmanship. Strive to be the talk of the league for the class with which you carry yourselves.

A COUPLE WEEKS before the playoffs, we took the team to a tournament. The tournament had some very good teams entered and we felt it would prove to be an excellent test for our team. We had already secured third place in our league and we had no room to move up or down, so as a coaching staff we were concerned about the lack of meaningful games heading into the play-offs. This tournament was perfect for us.

In our first game of the tournament we played very well and we were able to win by a score of 5-0. The nice part about the win was that we had five different scorers. Each line scored a goal and Carter scored a beautiful goal jumping into the rush.

In our second game, we were in a dogfight. It was our best effort of the season, we had excellent contributions from everyone, and I thought it was easily Blake's best game of the year. He made some outstanding stops early in the game when we needed him. For a 0-0 game well into the third it was quite entertaining and AJ scored the winner with under two minutes remaining in the game.

The third game of the tournament was a seesaw battle, with our opponent jumping out to an early 2-0 first period lead. Adam scored to start the rally early in the second and Zack and AJ scored to take us into the third with a 3-2 lead. The game was tied early in the third and on the next shift after surrendering the tying goal Sammy joined the rush and finished a pass from AJ to score the game winner. Brock scored an empty netter to win 5-3.

The fourth game saw Teddy assert himself with two early goals and Reese added a short-handed goal as we cruised to a 3-1 win. Our defense played their best game of the season. It was beautiful to watch them set screens for each other, use their partners, and join the attack. They really dominated with their decisions with the puck; I don't think they turned the puck over once the entire game.

In the Semi-Finals, we were in for another nail-biter. We had never played the team we were playing before that game. Naturally, there was a feeling out process and then they got the early jump. They pressured and outnumbered us all over the ice. They were the most relentless fore-checking team we had played all year. We had all kinds of difficulty handling their pressure and their cycle. If it weren't for Ricky the game would have been over after the first period. In the second period we encouraged Ricky to get out and play the puck to help our defense handle their fore-check. With Ricky's help, we were able to counter them with some great speed in the Neutral Zone and we mounted an attack of our own. It was a tight game deep into the third period when AJ made a brilliant pass to Cain who scored the winner with five minutes to go.

This was Cain's second MVP award of the tournament. In the key moments of the game when we needed a goal, he just raised his game and played at another level. It was something to watch.

As we were returning to the locker room after the game, Cain pulled me aside just before the door and asked if he could say something before I addressed the team. Of course, I obliged and we followed him in.

We got everyone's attention and Cain stood up to speak to the team.

He said, "The person who thought I should get this MVP award obviously didn't see the first period when Ricky kept us in it. If it wasn't for him, there is no way we would have won. Ricky you deserve this award more than me and I think you should have it."

Everyone was stunned and all eyes in the room shifted to Ricky. Ricky just shook his head no, more in disbelief than rejecting the gesture.

Cain walked over to Ricky, handed him the award, and shook his hand. Every player in the room stood up and cheered wildly.

It didn't matter what happened in the Finals after seeing something like that. We had already won.

Nevertheless, we were pumped for the Finals. We felt like the team of destiny, as a few breaks went our way early in the game. We jumped out to a 2-1 lead at the end of the first.

This was the quickest pace we had played during the tournament. It wasn't a physical game at all, it was more of a speed game and the two teams were evenly matched. The goalies were outstanding and the game looked to be ours, that is, until our luck ran out.

Brownie was skating the puck around the net in our own zone with one of their players in pursuit. Brownie was just getting ready to make a pass when he had his top hand elbow hooked and he lost control of the puck. At the speed he was skating he over-skated the puck and the opponent picked up the loose puck and walked in and scored. That goal tied the game with under five minutes to go.

The momentum of the game clearly swung in their favor and they continued to apply more pressure. With less than two minutes to go they got a fortunate bounce at the blue line. They raced in on a two-on-one and scored what proved to be the tournament-winning goal.

As a team, we were disappointed. We played well enough to win, but we needed one more break and it wasn't meant to be.

Our custom in games like this was that each of our players would meet each player on their team at the presenter to congratulate them before they received their award. We found it was a great way to show class whether we won or lost.

One by one, players on our team took turns to congratulate their players before their trophy presentation, except for one.

Brownie, apparently still stinging over the play that led to the tying goal, didn't go up to congratulate his assigned player. I didn't notice it at the time, but Bud pointed it out to me afterwards. I wished that I had known sooner, but by the time Bud told me we were already in the room.

As soon as I heard, I sent Tony in to tell Brownie to meet me in the stands after he was changed.

All I could think about was the morning game when Cain showed unbelievable sportsmanship and class, and just a few hours later Brownie was doing the complete opposite.

When Brownie met me in the stands, he thought he knew what I wanted to talk about. He started by saying "I'm sorry coach about that play. I thought he deserved a penalty for that hook."

"Brownie," I said, "I didn't call you out here to talk about the play you made. I'm more concerned about what you didn't do."

"What do you mean coach?" Brownie asked.

"What does our team do in every game where there is a presentation win or lose?" I asked.

"Oh, I know what you are going to say. I was just pissed off about how we lost," Brownie tried to explain.

"I don't care how we lost the game, I care about how we react in those situations and I didn't like what you did. You chose to let your own disappointment get in the way of showing class. I'm really disappointed that you allowed yourself to do that. In whatever situation that occurs, no matter how bad you think you were treated, or how disappointed you are in the result, you must always present yourself with class," I said sternly to emphasize my point.

"I understand coach, I know now what I should have done, and I will react differently next time," Brownie assured.

"Good, let's learn from this and become better for it," I encouraged.

"Thanks Coach," Brownie said knowingly.

No matter what happens on the ice, I want my team to carry themselves with class. Brownie is a great kid and I know he just let his emotions get the best of him.

COACHING CHALLENGE #32: PROMOTING SPORTSMANSHIP

1. Detail an example of great sportsmanship that you have witnessed in hockey.
2. Detail an example of poor sportsmanship that you have witnessed in hockey.
3. What are three ways your team can consistently demonstrate class and sportsmanship?

33

The Final Series

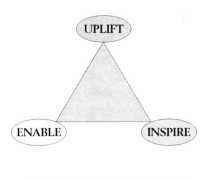

WE HAD ADVANCED through the playoffs only to meet the defending league champions in the finals.

We weren't able to beat this team in three tries this season, but our last game against them was nearly two months ago. This was a huge test for our team; we had overcome so much during the season being in this position was a wonderful opportunity and a great reward for our hard work. I don't think any of us expected to be there in the end, so there was a relaxed feeling amongst our group.

Before the playoffs, we did a couple of powerful team building activities to sharpen our focus. We did an exercise that I would recommend to any team heading into the playoffs.

We gave the players cue cards and for each player they were asked to write down one reason or story that made them thankful that this person was their teammate. We got the team together and we formed a half circle with a chair in the middle. One-by-one each player on the team was on the hot seat in the middle of the half circle and each of his teammates would take turns reading their reason or story about that person.

Then we had an old treasure chest that Bud had, and we spray-painted it in our team colors. Bud then painted our team slogan on the lid.

"The strength of the pack is the wolf, and the strength of the wolf is the pack."

Then we glued our hand framework to the inside bottom of the chest reminding us of our team structure.

After the hot seat exercise, we gave each player a copy of his cue cards that listed all the reasons why he was important and we had each player put the cue cards into the chest.

Forrest said that he would bring the chest to every game. I was interested to see how they would respond to the chest. I was hoping it would be a source of inspiration to them, a reminder to play for one another.

After we won the first game of the playoffs in the first round, Forrest picked up the game puck and brought it into the room. He told Bud that he wanted to put a screw through the puck and attach it right to the chest. They started to keep the puck from every game that they won and attached it to the chest. They had a place reserved for 12 pucks, the number of wins we would need to win the championship.

We had been awarding the team work boots to the hardest working player on the team each game all season long. Now because each winner would sign the boots, there wasn't a lot of room on the boots for the playoffs. The team decided that for the playoffs the hardest working player would sign the chest instead. The kids made up their own private ceremony after each play-off game for the 'official signing.' They were totally into it and it was neat to watch the chest evolve into a real symbol.

We made our way through each round, and with each victory, our team became stronger. We noticed that different players were stepping up their game and playing their best games of the season when it counted the most.

While there was a different player that caught our eye each game, there were times when we were fighting hard to resist the old habits.

One game we were behind in the third period and we noticed the kids were starting to get more individual; they were pressing and forcing plays, gradually pulling away from the system. With five minutes to go, Bud suggested that I take a time-out to refocus the group. I just tried to point out that we didn't need a hero, what we needed was a group effort. After the time-out, the puck started to move again and we were able to pull out the win.

Now that we were going into the final series to determine the league champion, we didn't know what to expect.

The hard fought series was extremely physical; every inch of the ice contested. It was awesome to watch our players compete at this level.

We won game one and lost game two and game three. Our backs were against the wall heading into game four.

Not even a minute into game four AJ took a vicious two-hand slash across the wrists and it was clear to everyone that he was hurt. He tried to play through it, but he just wasn't the same. He had a hard time handling the puck and much of his shooting strength was compromised. We needed someone to step up.

On nearly every other team in the league Adam would be the go-to-guy, but on our team, he had to play in AJ's shadow. AJ drew all the attention; he played against the other team's top players or their top pests. Adam was an outstanding player in his own right, but couldn't be compared to AJ, so he was often overlooked and underappreciated.

That was until game four. With AJ hurting and the uncertainty about whether or not he could even play, it was Adam's time to emerge from the background.

I don't think Adam ever looked at it like he was in AJ's shadow, I think he just enjoyed playing hockey, and he viewed AJ as a friend.

When AJ was hurt, Adam jumped to the forefront. With each shift that went by he became more assertive, more determined and more of a factor. He started to carry the team through a tough second period. Blake was playing incredible hockey as well, but Adam continued to get better and better as the game went on.

It was 1-1 early in the third when Adam took over. First he ran over the defenseman on the fore-check and jumped off the wall for a jam play at the net that drew a crowd and left a loose puck in the crease for Zack to score.

Then a couple shifts later Adam caught the puck with speed in the neutral zone and drove the puck wide carrying the defenseman to the net and drawing a penalty.

On the ensuing power play he had a great second effort to keep the puck alive in the zone. He executed a perfect high give-go with Sammy, and whizzed a one-timer to the back of the net.

After we scored the power play goal, we just knew we were going to get the next penalty and with Reese in the box, Robbie needed to step up on the penalty kill. Robbie responded by intercepting a pass on the breakout and holding the puck down low in their zone killing precious moments off the man advantage.

Brock picked up a puck in the neutral zone late in a shift, and dumped it in for a change, which was wonderful to see.

Carter was physical in his own zone, pinning the puck carrier on a couple occasions creating a loose puck and a turnover in our favor.

It was fitting that Blake made the last stop of the game as time expired and we won to force a fifth and deciding game.

34

CHAMPIONSHIP GAME

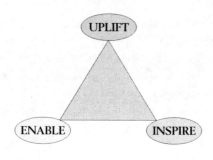

STRATEGY #33: ENJOY EVERY MOMENT

It is always the little things and the unexpected that matter the most. There will be countless breakthroughs that your players will experience during the year. Be on the lookout for them as they make it all worthwhile.

BUD, TONY AND I jumped into the car to head to the rink for the Championship game. There was a big decision that was weighing on all of us. We agonized over the decision all night and the conversation over breakfast would decide it.

The decision was who to start in net. Blake had come so far this year. He has established himself as a legitimate number 1 goaltender. His performance in game four not only earned my trust, but also the confidence of the team. I thought most everyone that surrounded the team was expecting me to go back to him. It seemed natural to go with the hot hand. The only problem was I felt uncomfortable. Ricky had also grown rapidly this year and he had been our go-to goalie all season long and now we were faced with the championship game and all of a sudden I didn't believe in him. I wasn't comfortable with that. He was a competitor, probably more-so than everyone else on the team. His competitive spirit was a double-edged sword at times, but I had an ace in the hole.

Tony was Ricky's coach, but Bud knew how to get players prepared to play. Over breakfast, I listened to both Bud and Tony make their case for Blake. Blake had earned the opportunity they said. I agreed, but Ricky was our goalie all year; this was not the time to take it out of his hands. I decided we needed to go with Ricky, and Bud and Tony were going to make sure he was ready. Blake had proven all he needed to prove; it was Ricky's time.

As we pulled into the parking lot of the arena well over an hour before game-time, as had become our coaches' ritual, we noticed Kyle standing at the front doors.

Bud said, "Look there's a kid who is ready to play."

Kyle was a boy who had to redefine his game to re-establish himself at this level. He took the fact that he was cut from the team as a personal wake-up call. Everyone was so impressed at his attitude and willingness to work hard at the parts of his game that let him down so hard during tryouts. Most kids would have been bitter, looked for excuses, and blamed us for not making the team. In his mind, he never stopped being part of this team and I believe that's why he made the team the following year.

When we jumped out of the car and made our way up to the front doors, Kyle met us halfway and said, "Hey, good luck today. We can do it. We can beat these guys," he said with clenched teeth. Even though he was not playing you could see the competitiveness bubbling over.

Kyle didn't know that I called his Dad the night before to call him up to play for us in the Championship game. He was stunned when I asked him, "Did you bring your equipment Kyle?"

His face dropped, "Yes, I think it's still in my Dad's car."

"I think it would mean a lot to the guys if you would dress and play for us tonight. I mean you are here anyways, why watch the game from the stands when you can be right there with us?" I said wondering if he would even want to.

"Wow, that's unbelievable coach, I'd love to," Kyle said as his eyes welled up with tears of joy.

"You know Kyle, the way you have responded to what happened to you this year speaks very well of the kind of character you have. You have championship character and a championship attitude. I think we need as much of that on our team as we can get. You earned a chance to be with these guys, so get your gear, you're playing tonight!" I said trying to find a way to show how impressed I was with him.

He didn't need to be asked twice. He ran into the building to find his Dad. His excitement told me right away that it was the right thing to do.

Bud reached over to put his hand on my shoulder and said, "That kid just grew two feet."

The next problem was AJ. We had not received word about his wrist. I feared the worst, but hoped for the best. No matter whether he could play or not, his own character and will to win had transcended his unbelievable talent.

When he came through the locker room door with his hockey bag over his shoulder, we knew he was going to play. Who knew what his hand would allow him to be capable of? At that point, I didn't care; I was thrilled that everyone was healthy enough to at least suit up for the last game. AJ was hurting; you could see it in his eyes. His wrist was in bad shape, but he came to play today and that alone was inspiration to us all.

We got to just under a half hour to game time which was when we usually started pulling kids into one-on-ones to focus them on their game and let them know that we believed in them. I was never one for speeches before the game, up until this point I hadn't made a pre-game locker room speech the entire year. We always addressed the kids either in one-on-ones or in lines and defense pairs.

By addressing the kids in small groups or one-on-one all year we got a chance to learn how each player prepared himself for the game and allowed him to find his own a routine of preparation. If they needed me to go in the room before every game to inspire them to play, they were playing for the wrong reasons. Besides how many "one for the gipper" speeches could I really do during the season? I knew that would wear thin pretty quick.

The other nice thing that happened was the kids started to stand up and make speeches of their own. Once they realized that I wasn't going to make speeches before games, Forrest began to take it upon himself to get his team ready. The leadership that he was able to show in the dressing room before each game transferred directly onto the ice in games and in practice. When Forrest spoke, everyone listened. He earned a tremendous amount of respect that way. When different kids stood up to say their peace, they made themselves accountable. How can a player stand up and preach hard work and discipline, and then go on the ice with a lackluster effort and take lazy penalties?

From the minute the game was underway, Kyle was involved. He praised every player for every shift the entire game. He didn't miss anyone. With AJ injured, I was able to get Kyle quite a few shifts early in the game. It was rewarding to watch him compete so well at this level. I remember seeing Coach

Black in the corner of the rink watching the game, and thinking about his invaluable role in helping Kyle get back to this level.

Both teams looked nervous, neither played particularly well in the first period. I think we had three good chances to score in the period and they had two. It was a feeling out process and I was hoping we'd be the team to settle down first. I felt the first goal was critical in a game like this.

AJ had a couple good shifts early, but he just didn't have the strength in his wrist to finish plays. He was getting frustrated and I knew I just needed to keep encouraging him and keep him in the moment, something would break his way it always did.

Teddy worked hard going to the net and he set three beautiful screens at the side of the net for chances to score. He got his hands on a rebound late in the second and rung it off the post.

Ricky was stellar, he hadn't faced a lot of action through the first two periods, but he had to make two tough stops on their power play which helped keep the momentum from tipping in their direction.

About a minute into the third period, Cain took a hard hit to chip the puck out sending Teddy and Carter on a two on one. Carter had jumped into the play from his position in front of the net. As soon as he saw Cain skating for the chip he took off. His timing was perfect. As Teddy took the offensive blue line he saw Carter joining him and gave him the puck. Carter didn't hesitate he one-timed the puck into the net to open the scoring. Our bench erupted and it was tough to get them to refocus. The hardest shift to play is the one after you score a big goal.

Two shifts later, they began to press for the equalizer. We were playing hard, but just hanging on. They worked the puck down low very well against us. They had generated a couple chances to score. We had just chipped the puck out the zone and tried to sneak in a line change. Bubba was dying out there and he struggled to make it to the bench. They turned the chipped puck up ice and head-manned it quickly. Sammy was trying hard to get back in the play but he was too far way. Just when it looked like they were going to get a clean chance, Reese came out of nowhere to hunt the player down and make a diving play to knock the puck away. We thought it was a clean play, but the ref called him for tripping.

On the ensuing power play, they banged home a rebound to tie the game at one.

In the third period I had taken AJ off every defensive zone face-off, he was struggling with strength in the circle so I had Reese and Adam take the draws. Early in overtime, we faced a defensive zone face off and the coach motioned for his weak-side defenseman to line up at the top of the circle in offensive zone face-off. Their center then jumped the face-off and the linesman threw both centers out of the circle. That meant AJ would have to take the draw. Reese turned to me on the bench and said, "Coach, look at how low their defenseman is. We should do the blast face-off play."

We had worked on the blast face-off periodically during the season, but without much success. Now I had AJ in the circle and there wasn't time to make the adjustment.

On the ensuing face-off, AJ was beat cleanly on the draw and #6 got a shot on goal. Ricky stopped and held the puck for another face-off. I immediately made the line change and sent Reese out with Brock and Robbie.

Reese went straight to Sammy and positioned him at the bottom of the circle, then gave Robbie a telling nod signifying it was time to go.

Reese won the face-off cleanly and Sammy sent the puck off the far wall. Robbie was in full flight when he picked up the puck at the red line. Brock had joined the play and created a 2 on 1 rush to the net. Our bench stood up.

Robbie hit the blue-line and passed to Brock who was on his strong side. Brock wound up for a shot. The defenseman started to drop towards Brock's stick. At the last moment, just as the defenseman was about to hit the ice, Brock faked the shot and slid the puck under the sliding defenseman to Robbie who was still going to the net.

Robbie was shocked to see the puck come out from under the defenseman and just tried to get a stick on the puck. He continued skating to the post and got his stick on it to beat the goalie who was sliding over. When the puck hit the back of the net, we froze on the bench. Still trying to process what had just happened. Robbie raised his stick in the air and Brock jumped into his arms. It was at that moment we realized we had just won. The bench erupted with joy. The kids were hugging each other as they scrambled over the boards to race to the other end to join the celebration. Ricky was skating wildly up the middle of the ice. Bubba tried to grab him to hug him, but Ricky continued skating on a mission to join the team in the corner of the rink as the team piled onto one another in celebration.

Bud leaned over and shook my hand, I was still in shock, and Tony joined us as we huddled on the bench to enjoy the moment.

As we broke away from our embrace, we saw Forrest reach into the net to grab the game winning puck.

The opposing coaches had come to our bench to congratulate us. We shook hands and then made our way to the corner where the kids were still bouncing with elation. The dramatic ending to the game had created such an overwhelming feeling for all of us. We couldn't believe what just happened. It all seemed like a dream.

We made our way to the blue-line for the championship presentation and watched as the first opposing player made his way to the presenter to receive his trophy and Brownie was the first to skate over to shake his hand. It was wonderful to watch Brownie as he continued to skate down the opposing blue-line to shake hands with each of his opponents that day. To lead the group like that showed he had grown from the earlier tournament.

I stood on the blueline beside our bench as the ceremony continued and watched as our players skated proudly one-by- one to the trophy presenter, shaking hands with him in anticipation of receiving the award marking their achievement and posing momentarily while their pictures were taken.

As each player skated forward, a specific moment from the season would appear in my mind framing the teaching moment that defined my relation-ship with each player. There was the time when Forrest stepped on the ice the first practice as captain and tapped his stick three times sending the team full speed around the ice. Then there was the moment with Cain in the bleachers when he made a commitment to become a more complete player, and just moments ago when Brock passed the puck on the 2 on 1 to Robbie making a commitment to be a team player. As each player skated forward, a different moment appeared in my mind. I realized then that the *purpose* of coaching was to UPLIFT, ENABLE and INSPIRE. The season was instantly reduced in my mind to a series of special moments and what they represented to me and to the player. The choices, actions and impact made in those moments would determine whether I would be fondly remembered or wistfully forgotten.

"Coach!" Tony said, touching my shoulder. "The kids are ready for the team picture."

Once we got back into the locker room, Forrest came out of the room and said "give me a minute coach before you get started."

I nodded and followed him into the room.

Forrest stood up and held the game-winning puck in his hand. He paused to hold back his emotion. Then he started to speak.

"I just wanted to say that I want to give the game puck to someone who de-serves to be recognized. This puck goes to a guy who made a great unselfish play, when most everyone in this room probably would have just taken the shot. I want this game winning goal puck to go to Brock."

The team erupted in cheers as Forrest stood in front of Brock, presented him with the puck, and extended his hand in congratulations. Brock accepted the puck and looked at Forrest's hand; he hesitated and then bypassed his hand and hugged him.

The team gathered in the middle of the room for one last time as Brock signed the chest.

What a perfect ending to the season. Bud, Tony and I made our way around the room congratulating each of the players individually, and as the door closed behind us we could hear the sound of those seventeen kids singing for the last time as a team, Champions!

35

PERFECT

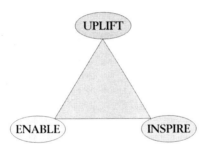

STRATEGY #34: REMEMBER YOUR PURPOSE

There are few things in life more rewarding than the satisfaction of knowing you were a positive influence in the life of a child and your impact extends well beyond the playing field. Seize the opportunity and own it; be someone worth remembering.

HOW DOES A coach pursue a perfect season in youth sports? What would be the elements that define it? What would your players say would be the perfect season for them?

In the years that followed, I reflected many times on the moments that created that season. It was my first year of coaching and it shaped my coaching philosophy for the years that followed.

I went into my first season of coaching excited about all the things I wanted to teach the kids about hockey. I didn't realize at the time that years later the things I would remember most were the moments, the laughter, the breakthroughs in character development and the lessons they taught me.

I learned that the impact a coach can have on a hockey team is only limited to his desire to turn the many challenging situations that occur in competition into investments that build the character of the people underneath the equipment.

Hockey is a microcosm of life. It is a playground where kids learn personal discipline, dedication, determination, work ethic, teamwork, sacrifice and resourcefulness. Hockey is a place that helps them build confidence, make friends and learn to lead.

Hockey is all those things for me; I just didn't realize it until I became a coach. That's when I began to reflect on the coaches that I had had, and engaged in conversations with our area's best and most influencing coaches. The funny thing is, when you reminisce about a favorite coach or a favorite teacher, why does one person stand above everyone else? You don't remember them for the subject they taught, you remember them for the way they made you feel about yourself.

They had a way to uplift, enable and inspire you to perform at your very best. They cared enough to bring out the best in you and those around you.

Some day everyone will become a coach to someone in his or her life. My hope is each of you chooses to rise above the context of your subject and make a positive impact on a young person who needs you to be more than a coach.

Appendix 1: Coaching Strategies

STRATEGY #1: COACH TO MAKE A DIFFERENCE
Discover as much reward in the development process of each player as you do in the competitive results of your team.

STRATEGY #2: LEAD FROM BEHIND
Control for a coach comes from accountability. You will find no greater accountability measure for your team than the one those you are leading prescribe for themselves.

STRATEGY #3: PLAN TO TEACH
Lasting and impacting development is progressive. Identify the elements that must be taught and teach them in order.

STRATEGY #4: THE BEST TEACHING MOMENTS COME AT UNEXPECTED TIMES
Create a habit of engaging in conversation with your players, many times simply asking a question to a young player will lead you into a perfect teaching moment.

STRATEGY #5: SURROUND YOUR PLAYERS WITH THE BEST RESOURCES
Take the time to recruit complementary staff that will create value to the team, the players and be a credit to your association.

STRATEGY #6: PLAYER EVALUATION PLAN
Having a clear evaluation plan will create order and purpose to your tryouts. Order and purpose provide the opportunity to properly evaluate and ultimately select.

STRATEGY #7: CREATE EVALUATION SITUATIONS
For players who are on "the bubble" take the time to create situations in the tryouts to provide them the chance to play their way onto the team.

STRATEGY #8: ONE CHANCE TO MAKE A FIRST IMPRESSION
Plan and execute your first team practice to reflect the way you want your team to approach and perform during practice all season.

STRATEGY #9: SELECT YOUR TEAM AND CONTINUE TO INSPIRE THE DREAM
In the moment when a player is most disappointed lies an opportunity to uplift, enable and inspire. Don't miss it. It could be the only one you get!

STRATEGY #10: BUILD A TEAM OR A CULTURE
Everybody's desire for acceptance and belonging creates the conditions for each of your players to bond as a team.

STRATEGY #11: SET TANGIBLE INDIVIDUAL AND TEAM GOALS
Create a system to measure development and provide an opportunity for your players to achieve success on multiple levels.

STRATEGY #12: CREATE A STARTING POINT
Create ground zero, design an improvement plan and involve the family in the program. This sets a natural improvement chart that motivates all to stay the course.

STRATEGY #13: ENCOURAGE PERFECTION, PRAISE EXCELLENCE
Where kids are concerned, you get what you ask for and your team will play the way you practice, therefore demand and praise quality practice habits.

STRATEGY #14: BE YOUR TEAM'S ROLE MODEL OF CLASS AND RESPECT.
You will only get respect if you are willing to give it.

STRATEGY #15: DEVELOP LEADERS
While there can only be one captain on a hockey team, look for ways for all of your players to be in leadership positions at various points during the season.

STRATEGY #16: UTILIZE AND MANIPULATE TIME AND SPACE IN PRACTICE
Continually challenge your players' ability by reducing and manipulating the time and space they have to work in.

STRATEGY #17: CHALLENGE TALENT
Work hard to ensure the top end of your team is always being pushed to get better.

STRATEGY #18: LEAVE NO ONE BEHIND
Take a teaching approach to challenges. A teacher is always looking for ways to reach their students more effectively.

STRATEGY #19: IMPROVE STICK SKILLS
Knowing what hand players shoot and knowing what hand is their dominant hand in life, is the first step to building elite stick skill.

STRATEGY #20: DEVELOP THE THREE SKILL SPEEDS OF HOCKEY
Invest in the three skill speeds, focusing on developing the skill speed in combination; they are fundamental to expanding their ability to perform at the next level.

STRATEGY #21: DEVELOP THE COMPLETE PLAYER
Make it a priority to ensure that all players can play in all situations. Versatility is a wonderful gift any coach can give his players.

STRATEGY #22: CHALLENGE PLAYERS TO PLAY DIFFERENT POSITIONS
Expand the potential of a player on your team by experimenting to reveal the position/role that best suits his strengths.

STRATEGY #23: INSPIRE BY SHOWING CONFIDENCE FIRST.
Be on the lookout for ways to show confidence in your players; you never know how they will reward your faith.

STRATEGY #24: USE TRIANGLES TO TEACH OFFENSIVE AWARENESS.
Offensive hockey is all about triangles. Teach your players to understand and manipulate triangles and you teach them offensive support.

STRATEGY #25: USE VIDEO AS A TEACHING TOOL.
A picture is worth a thousand words.

STRATEGY #26: DEVELOP OFF-ICE PREPARATION AND TRAINING HABITS.
Link off-ice work habits to on-ice performance.

STRATEGY #27: MONITOR YOUR PLAYERS' INTERNAL DIALOGUE
Focus is about staying in the moment. Work hard to keep your players' attention to the *now*, not what was.

STRATEGY #28: ONE PLAYING FOR FOUR OR FOUR PLAYING FOR ONE?
Put a premium on players moving without the puck, reward players who move with a purpose.

STRATEGY #29: REWARD EFFORT AND DETERMINATION
When you challenge a player and notice improvement in the effort and concentration put forth, make a point to encourage and reward.

STRATEGY #30: TEACH TIMING AS A SKILL
Contact is a skill best utilized inside the context of the game. The best body checkers are able to recognize a great hit opportunity without having to hunt for it.

STRATEGY #31: AN EDUCATION IS FOR LIFE
In the term 'student-athlete', the student comes first. Take an interest and become an advocate of balanced living and academic achievement.

STRATEGY #32: GAME RESPECT STARTS WITH YOU COACH
Hold your players to a high standard of sportsmanship. Strive to be the talk of the league for the class with which you carry yourselves.

STRATEGY #33: ENJOY EVERY MOMENT
It is always the little things and the unexpected that matter the most. There will be countless breakthroughs that your players will experience during the year. Be on the lookout for them as they make it all worthwhile.

STRATEGY #34: REMEMBER YOUR PURPOSE
There are few things in life more rewarding than the satisfaction of knowing you were a positive influence in the life of a child and your impact extends well beyond the playing field. Seize the opportunity and own it; be someone worth remembering.

ABOUT THE AUTHOR

DARRYL BELFRY IS a pioneer in hockey development. At 21 years of age, he founded **www.playmakershockey.com,** the first, and remains the only year-round hockey development company in the Niagara Region.

His teaching over the last 10 years has been instrumental in the development of many of the Niagara Region's best hockey players including 2003 NHL 3rd Overall, Nathan Horton of the Florida Panthers, Patrick Kane a projected 2007 NHL 1st Rounder and Daniel Girardi of the NY Rangers.

In 2005, Darryl became the first full-time Director of Coach and Player Development in the Alliance for Brantford Minor Hockey and has also been a coach mentor for Wainfleet Minor Hockey and Niagara-on-the-Lake Minor Hockey.

He has been a guest speaker at numerous coaching and hockey development seminars and workshops, including the Canisius College Coaching Symposium and is an Alliance Hockey Coach Facilitator. He is a NCCP certified advanced level coach, worked extensively with the men's team at Brock University and is a former head coach of the St. Catharines Falcons Junior Hockey Club.

Darryl, his wife Ruth and daughter Ella reside in Ridgeway Ontario.

CONTACT:

FOR INFORMATION ON how to book Darryl Belfry for a ...

- Coaching Development Seminars
- Player Development Seminars
- Organizational Consulting Opportunities
- Hockey Development Camps

for your association please visit *www.playmakershockey.com* or contact him directly at darryl@playmakershockey.com

ISBN 142512849-1